EIGHT-DAY RETREAT
with St Ignatius of Loyola

Norbert Alcover

EIGHT-DAY RETREAT
with St Ignatius of Loyola

Material for restructuring your life

 St Paul Publications

Original title: *Reestructurar la vida*
© 1989 Ediciones Paulinas, Madrid, Spain

Translated from the Spanish by Dinah Livingstone

Cover design by Diane Edward

St Paul Publications
Middlegreen, Slough SL3 6BT, United Kingdom

English translation © St Paul Publications UK 1991

ISBN 085439 388 9

Printed by The Guernsey Press Co. Ltd, Guernsey, C.I.

St Paul Publications is an activity of the priests and brothers of the Society of St Paul who proclaim the Gospel through the media of social communication

Contents

Foreword

The memory of Ignatius of Loyola has been revived with many different intentions and has always been present in the Church's history over the last few centuries. Now we have reached the fifth centenary of his birth (1591-1991), Ignatius has also inspired this book's author.

The reader will not find here either a commentary or a glossary on the text of the Spiritual Exercises. The author offers these pages as 'material' intended to be helpful for an eight-day spiritual experience. He recommends them to those who are familiar with the text of the Exercises, because they have tried them in one form or another, and to 'repeaters' of the experience – in the Ignatian sense of the term 'repetition' [62 and 118], who want to go more deeply into certain particularly important aspects of the Christian way by which the Spirit leads them.

This explains both the Ignatian style of the author's general outline and also the liberty he has taken with his method. These may appear contradictory but in Ignatian terms they are not.

The author's intentions are defined in three key words:
– *Material* to help you to co-operate in accepting God's initiatives. The material takes various forms: psalm-like prayers aiming to help you get into a prayerful mood; *reflections* to situate you in the context of the human and Christian mystery; directions and paths for prayers; suggestions for reviewing and examining what has happened during the experience.
– *Restructuring*, the word by which the author translates

the Ignatian 'ordering your life'. It is valid as long as we do not give it the reductionist interpretation of arranging, re-ordering 'things', pieces. It is life that has to be 'ordered', and ultimately that means personal relations.

– *Experience*. By this is meant experience of God, not just as an object but, principally, as the author of the experience itself. He does it. You accept it freely at your own centre, which becomes transformed and open. And you 'rid your-self of self-love, self-will and self-interest' [189], which is a 'sign' that salvation is coming. The book is intended for Christians who want to be witnesses and therefore need experience. Without experience there can be no witness.

All this can be used by the exerciser, particularly the experienced exerciser the book has in mind, through the selection of whatever is helpful. But no one can or should save oneself the trouble of personally selecting from the material offered. Or even, as is suggested, re-creating it for oneself. Guided by the Spirit, you can adjust the dose of personal listening to the Lord, which is the decisive factor, self-analysis (prayer through observation) of what is going on inside you, and discovery of new levels of the Gospel kingdom by which you feel attracted.

The author rightly stresses the appropriateness of con-stantly comparing all this experience and personalising it with the help of another 'witness', the director. Not even the most authentic of texts can serve as a substitute for this meeting of witnesses listening to the Lord, and letting your-self be led by the 'signs' that he gives you in the course of daily experience.

In these pages the conditions given for testing whether the experience is genuine are thoroughly Ignatian. The au-thor's effort to situate the daily Exercises in the context of our present historical reality is also Ignatian. The 'day-unit' given to each step of the experience is Ignatian and so are many of the practical recommendations, which translate some of the classical Ignatian 'additions'. The list of questions proposed for the reflections are Ignatian, and especially the suggestions given at the end of every exercise, which try to help the exerciser define himself or herself in terms of positions nearly always formulated as alternatives. The vision at the beginning and throughout the book of our creaturehood and essential dependency is Ignatian. From it derives the necessity to proceed from the start by means of free decisions that 'please' the Lord (Jn 8:29). There is the Ignatian reference to the determining nuclei of the Exercise process and there are various Ignatian commentaries on key points in this process.

Other Ignatian aspects go without saying and are easily identifiable by those to whom the method is familiar. We could dispute whether certain changes of methods introduced by the author are Ignatian, although they are legitimate for the author's stated purpose of helping the exerciser to learn. For example the treatment of the Two Flags, the King's Summons and the contemplation to attain love. We stress the importance of having the full Ignatian text. Obviously it is very practical to have it handy while doing the Exercises.

Even though the author does not say so, it is obvious that this material can easily be adapted for Exercises in ordinary life [19]. Of course these are even more in need of help from a director, that is, another 'witness' to the same person, Jesus the Lord, and to the same task, of proclaiming God the Father continually (i.e., making his presence felt).

At this moment in our history we need to abandon the frivolity of fads and fashions and come home to ourselves. This is where we can find salvation, as long as we keep open house and make it a home for others too. Anything that helps us to do this performs a useful service towards making us become more human and more Christian. That is why this book should be welcomed.

May the Lord bless the author's intention and make it fruitful: to help us re-order (restructure) our hearts, by allowing ourselves, in an Ignatian way, to be 'moved and possessed by God our Lord'.

Ignacio Iglesias, SJ

Matters to be discussed
on the evening before the exercises

Practical introduction

Theological and spiritual notes on the Ignatian
Exercises

Conditions for doing the Exercises in the way Ignatius
intended

On the thirteen propositions

Practical introduction

Christians today are recovering the necessary spiritual dynamism to proclaim Jesus Christ in our society. The postconciliar period got rid of a certain deadweight of spiritualism, with which we were encumbered. But in our concern for the primary importance of a faith of witness and involvement, we began to lose sight of the urgent need to keep a permanent deep, personal and communal experience of the God of Jesus Christ in the Spirit, as the basis of all witness and involvement. I think that nowadays this situation has begun to find a better balance. This is the context for the subject matter of this book.

I say subject matter. And indeed what follows is 'spiritual subject matter': to reorganise our lives in accordance with the living example of the Lord. On the one hand, the thirteen propositions which give the book its shape follow the rhythm of salvation history. But this rhythm is also dominated by the internal dynamism of the most relevant propositions in the Spiritual Exercises. Thus the book proposes a spiritual readjustment in terms of Ignatius of Loyola's own inner experience; we take the elements of his spirituality which are most suited to our way of thinking today. The numbers in brackets which are not given any particular explanation correspond to the numbers in the Spiritual Exercises.

By using this material – covering the period from creation to the Church – we set out a set of Eight-Day Exercises, following a traditional method which has given excellent results in the Church. These are not the actual month-long Exercises as they were originally conceived by Ignatius of

Loyola, neither are they just two or three days of 'spiritual retreat' which are not long enough for any encounter in depth with the Lord. It is not difficult for anyone today to set aside this week to devote to reshaping their life in an atmosphere of prayer and silence.

Having said this, here is an important and typically Ignatian warning. Ignatius regarded the task of discernment carried out by the exerciser and director together just as important as meditation and contemplation on the actual subjects proposed in the Exercises. The point is to reorganise your life and this means serenely reflecting to find out what God wants of you here and now. This is a complex task which helps you see your way forward more clearly... from the Lord's point of view. This does not mean that these Exercises cannot be done on your own. But a director is important, especially to help you 'discern and choose'.

I conclude this introduction with a few practical remarks:

1. This book is for believers of all kinds to use as they see fit, either for the classical eight-day exercises or to support any other spiritual experience. However, they contain some explicit references to the 'consecrated life'.

2. At the end of each of the thirteen propositions into which the material is divided, we give suggestions for particular reflection. These are intended to be an aid to assimilating the material. Each person will decide individually whether these suggestions are a help or a hindrance. If they are a hindrance, leave them out.

3. We suggest a rule for the conduct of the Exercises. As there is a lot of material here, the exerciser (or director) should select the elements most appropriate for the task, without worrying that leaving some out will harm the outcome. This means that all prayer periods must be well prepared.

4. All the material is equally useful for doing eight days of exercises alone. It could also be of use to someone directing a group of exercisers (as we have already said). In both cases see the preceding paragraph about selecting from the material.

5. The following details will be helpful in organising the eight days well:

— The day should begin with an introduction to the day's subject matter by a few words from the director (when there is one) and reading of the corresponding prayer. This will focus the day.

— The whole day is devoted to prayer, with talks by the director or individual reading of the material. Each person should try to organise time in a way that is both demanding and pleasant.

— The Eucharist should be celebrated at the end of the day as a moment of prayer in common, and it will be helpful if, after the appropriate readings, participants speak about their personal spiritual experiences during the day. In a group gathering, realising that the Lord is acting upon everyone taking part is a very effective way of encouraging each individual to go on.

— Needless to say, the only two books necessary for the week are the Bible and the Spiritual Exercises of St Ignatius. But each person doing the exercises may consult other works that are helpful... as long as they are not distracting.

I think these remarks are sufficient as an introduction to this week of exercises, which, as I have said, can be done alone but better in the company of a good director. Practising this yearly reorganisation of our life can act as a necessary antidote to the spiritual exhaustion so many of us feel in our work of proclaiming the kingdom. At the end of these Exercises we should feel refreshed, ready to tell our contemporaries about God's wonders and give an account of our hope.

After this practical introduction, here are some theological and spiritual notes on the Ignatian Exercises, so that we can approach the material with a clearer understanding.

Theological and spiritual notes on the Ignatian Exercises

The Spiritual Exercises of Ignatius of Loyola represent a deep and lasting personal experience of his own. Through experience Ignatius discovered the way to find God's will for himself. We catch a glimpse of this crucial experience in his autobiography. He passed from a 'disordered life' (especially in his 'affections') to a new 'ordered life', which conformed with salvation history.

Likewise, doing the exercises today means we are prepared to face up to ourselves seriously, seeking God's will for us, in a calm but exacting way. Each of us (even though we may not realise it) needs an urgent and thorough restructuring, to order the various elements of our lives in an appropriate Christian way.

First and foremost the Exercises are a movement of the spirit by the Spirit, an inner readjustment, a surrender and opening up to a new spiritual personality capable of serving God with all our might. This is what we mean when we speak of 'personal experience'.

Of course the stimulus to do this comes from a vivid realisation of our precarious situation as believers. Those who think they already have a firmly established and settled spiritual life, based on a set of unalterable certainties, are not called to undertake the Ignatian Exercises. Such persons will never manage to meet their call to profound personal conversion to truth and life, and may even be disappointed, because following this road does not bring new elements of self sufficiency. Restructuring means a previous taking to pieces. This is how Ignatius expects us to cope with our sinfulness.

So doing the Exercises is a strong challenge you set yourself: opening yourself to the possibility of God intervening in your life, so that you can change it completely in all its aspects. God imposing his fatherly will in an ongoing process of conscious choices. If you are not prepared for this dangerous intervention of our only Lord in your everyday life you had better not take on the experience of the Exercises. So we realise that the right word for this undertaking is risk. We risk all we are and have and desire... so that the Lord may restructure everything his way. The object of this process, which goes on afterwards in everyday life, is the Pauline new human being whom Jesus speaks of as being converted at the beginning of Mark's Gospel (cf Mk 1:15).

In a word, through listening to God via a process clearly indicated in the Spiritual Exercises, we start transforming our actual life, putting our passions in order, changing our character, and eventually becoming more Christian. This requires self-surrender, work, prayer and trust. Strictly speaking, Ignatian methodology is simply a way to the Gospel experience under another name: Christ's paschal mystery is human fullness.

Conditions for doing the Exercises in the way Ignatius intended

1. *Overall goal*

In a time of deep dismay but also anxious search by humanity, the Church, our communities and ourselves (a crisis in values, which affects our personal integrity), we need to re-experience the living basis of our faith in order to centre ourselves inwardly and thus restructure our lives in depth. This will allow us to give a reason for our hope. The

Exercises as presented to us by Ignatius are for this reordering of our life. At this point we should reread the prologue to the First Letter of John: the fundamental thing is personal experience of Jesus ('what we saw and felt with our hands'), but this experience urgently becomes a matter to proclaim ('what we saw and heard, we now declare to you'). For the believer all experience of God has an apostolic dimension. Therefore by restructuring our lives through a personal encounter with Jesus, the Exercises turn us into witnesses to the experience we have had.

2. *Necessary Ignatian attitudes recommended in the annotations* [1-20]

At the beginning of the Exercises, Ignatius gives twenty suggestions for doing them better, which are addressed both to 'those who give them and those who receive them'. We pick out three especially important annotations for guiding the whole experience:

– No. 5: *Self-surrender*: Place yourself wholly at stake, with great generosity, as if you previously did not have anything at all. Abandon any false security and let yourself be surprised by the Spirit of the Lord of the Church. He will open new horizons, which may be disconcerting but will mature your faith (Jn 3:5-8 and 1 Sam 3). The opposite of this self-surrender is to be closed in, not opening up to our Lord freely and generously. This is usually caused by fear (which is often irrational) of having to change our life. So the question is: when I begin the Exercises, do I detect in myself a willing attitude or a selfish closing up?

– No. 1: *Receptivity*: The definition of the Exercises given by Ignatius in Note 1 means we have to lay aside our particular worries that have a hold on us and welcome God's word in its renewing creativity. This creativity belongs to the Holy Spirit. It will very probably lead us along ways that are different from our current preoccupations, and as we said, will show us new goals. Nevertheless, if at the beginning there is some concern that is blocking our energy, it is wise to be aware of it and ask advice about it, because if not, it will dominate all the Exercises (Jn 1:12 and 4:1-42; Lk 5:1-11; Jer 1:4-19; Lk 1:26-38). So the question is: when I begin the Exercises, am I prepared completely to unblock, even though this may involve a painful decision?

– No. 18: *Personality*: Doing the Exercises involves thinking of a human being as a complete person, in which all the natural and Christian aspects are interrelated, forming a dialectical unity and making up our present personality. This means that if we judge ourselves to be 'something', we are judging this to be 'everything'. This way of thinking of the person involves risking everything, because it makes it impossible to keep back protected areas, in which we have built the idols we alone know about. This means rejecting both alienating spiritualism and immanent materialism (Mt 4:18-22; Lk 1:38 and 18:18-30). So the question is: when I begin the Exercises, am I prepared to stake and risk my whole person, or am I keeping back certain protected areas?

If you have difficulty with these three Ignatian conditions it is wise to consult a director of Exercises or some trustworthy person. Ask advice about whether you are in a state to do the Exercises without sabotaging them from the beginning. All this means that the introductory material requires a time of very demanding reflection.

3. *Practical starting point: checking our current image*

Our current image is the sum of our actions (doing), concerns (thinking), and wishes (wanting), which Ignatius calls 'affections' (as they are related to love). Comparing my present make-up with the Gospel qualities to be produced through the Exercises (Phil 2:12-13), I will have to modify my current image, making it more like the Gospel of Jesus. For this task it is not a bad idea to take a few notes at the beginning, describing my current image. Add to them as the experience progresses, in the context of an authentic 'discernment of spirits', both in accordance with Ignatius' attitude and the director's advice [313-336]. At the end of the Exercises we should have accumulated enough evangelical elements to remake our current image in accordance with God's will. This should enable us to reshape our whole personality. When we finish the Exercises it will be possible to draw up a sort of practical life plan for our life as a whole which should never be confused with a set of bleak regulations. We shall spend some time doing this on the last day.

Briefly, the important thing is that the person doing the Exercises should have a particular horizon, from the beginning, upon which to set all the material presented throughout the Exercises. If not, the Exercises lose their aim. Genuine Exercises are not just an experience of God but above all a profound restructuring of the person from within in terms of Ignatian choices. The essential and fixed reference point is the proclamation of the kingdom for love of Jesus Christ. Ignatius invites us to contemplate and this never means being passive but action in passion, allowing the will to be moved. All this makes us feel nervous today because it involves really changing our life. But Ignatius summons us with sharp insight to seek and find God's will.

4. *Tools of the Ignatian method*

Ignatius' wide experience and that of the great directors of the Exercises point to three necessary tools to make it a truly Ignatian experience:

4.1. *Silence*: Of course we can be with the Lord in any worldly situation but the Bible leads us to inner and outer silence as an atmosphere in which we can converse with God in a particularly intense and intimate way. Moreover, this necessary attention to our own inner life requires an absence of distractions, however positive these may be. There are days when we need to be by ourselves, alone with ourselves and our Lord. Note that it only needs one person in the group to talk out of place for the desirable atmosphere to be broken. Therefore silence must be stressed from the beginning, without question.

4.2. *Prayer:* It is hardly necessary to say that an encounter with ourselves and our Lord takes place in a context of prayer, a religious and never merely psychological context. Prayer is where all the potentialities of the exerciser meet to develop the experience. Therefore anything that helps sift out spurious elements from prayer will be very much taken into account in some of the Exercises (each person knows his or her individual hindrances to prayer). We should note from the beginning that although the task of reflection (what we commonly call 'meditation') is important in an experience of this kind, the task of contemplation is even more important. Contemplation involves the feelings more and this means that the will is radically moved to love (Jn 1:37-39; Annotation 2).

4.3. *Spiritual discernment:* Ignatius assumes from his own experience that such an experience provokes various fluctuations in the spirit. These must be analysed and compared, because they are showing us the presence of Jesus' spirit and the spirit of evil in our lives, or in other words, of love and selfishness (see most of the annotations). Hence the paramount importance of sharing all the 'motions' experienced with some person who understands the matter, in order to avoid both illusions and depressions, and above all to realise where the Spirit of the Lord Jesus is leading us. In the

Ignatian sense, prayer which does not lead to discernment leaves much to be desired. Because in the last resort what counts is restructuring, as a result of a free choice, and all this is a work of spiritual discernment. In doing the Exercises the most natural thing is to consult the director himself about spiritual fluctuations ([313-336] rules for spiritual discernment, and [169-189] matter relating to making choices).

4.5. *Permanent Petition:* Paul's words to his friends in Ephesus are completely appropriate to conclude this introduction, because they express a series of wishes that apply to anyone beginning the Exercises: "I pray that the God of our Lord Jesus Christ, the all-glorious Father, may confer on you the spiritual gifts of wisdom and vision, with the knowledge of him that they bring. I pray that your inward eyes may be enlightened, so that you may know what is the hope to which he calls you, how rich and glorious is the share he offers you among his people in their inheritance, and how vast are the resources of his power open to us who have faith" (Eph 1:17-19).

On the thirteen propositions

Our final preparatory task is to review rapidly the dynamic of the thirteen propositions, which are the backbone of this experience, while being very much aware of the four large parts into which the Exercises are divided. As we have already mentioned, these add up to a run-through of salvation history via its essential elements, but always viewed in the original light proposed by Ignatius in the Exercises. This is a useful task to enable the exerciser to understand from the beginning the whole of the material to be confronted, with its twofold biblical/Ignatian dimension. This is a task which can well be done either by the director or by the exerciser alone.

First day:
God's will and the meaning of life

Morning prayer. 'Prayer of the creature'.

Proposition for the whole day. 'Doing the Exercises':
God's fatherly will, the ultimate meaning of our life.
The 'existential questions'.

Prayer of the creature

Out of the depths I cry to you, Lord,
master of my whole existence,
which you brought about by a fatherly act of infinite love.

With the halting humility of a self-sufficient heart,
I accept you as beginning and end,
creator and fulfilment,
alpha and omega of everything I am and can be.

Accept this difficult surrender
and make it happy through the experience of your closeness,
until my joy consists in praising you by serving you,
transcending my own freedom through love.

You are my God who is present,
the God of my days,
who sounds me and knows me,
whom I seek as the heart seeks springs of living water.
You are my Father and I am your child:
this is the transforming reality of my whole existence.

Out of the depths I cry to you, Lord,
like a child who has fallen prey to disturbing fantasies,
who returns to the ultimate sources of his being
to go on living in serene fullness
and experience the joy of freedom
maturely surrendered.
Because a lot of walking disturbs the horizon.

Make my action a canticle of praise
and a filial service,
so that you may be blessed in me.
Make everything around me a path towards you
and as I go along it
let me make everything more divine because more human.

Make me walk among things
only as they lead me to you,
and make me treat them
in a way that makes them lead me ever more to you.
Strip me of everything by your love,
but make me nothing but love, as I am your image,
in an indifference arising from a deep reading
of reality.

Out of the depths I cry to you, Lord.
And I pray you to do your will,
which will make me a full human being,
in imitation of Jesus Christ, your blessed and favourite Son,
and in human history, of my brothers and sisters,
salvation history.

≈ ≈ ≈

Doing the Exercises: God's fatherly will as the ultimate meaning of our life

1. *Introduction* (First read the text slowly [23])

1.1. *The 'Ignatianism' of the principle and foundation*

It is obvious that we are living in a period which is very
unstable both in its values and emotions. This leads to a loss
of identity (radical inquiry as to who I am) and of emotional
balance (a sense of disintegration of my wishes). Moreover
there is a progressive elimination of the sacred in social life.

All this inevitably leads to the need to redefine our being and behaviour, which will be positive or negative according to our point of view. If we put it off any longer we risk being sucked into the secularist current surrounding us.

In this context Ignatius offers us his *anthropological vision of the cosmos*, defining the human by means of a radical self-confrontation. For him human beings must submit to the will of God, the Lord. So they must listen 'indifferently' and passionately to this will in freedom, given and taken, which is what makes us responsible for ourselves. Hence we find in all the Exercises and very particularly in the principle and foundation [23] a supply of dialectical material to restructure our believing life from a definite standpoint: the permanent and free choice of the divine will. We can call this 'Ignatianism': a particular way of being in the world and history as a responsible person living consistently with the mystery of our faith in God our Lord. In short, the doer of the Exercises, as defined in Ignatius' own words in the principle and foundation, is a person who has freely chosen the divine will. This means someone who was indifferent and has now been converted.

1.2. *Exercises for making choices*

This text [23] was begun in Manresa, like all the Exercises, but finalised in Paris and Rome, when Ignatius was in his full maturity. He sees it as a set of conditions making possible everything that follows in the rest of the book. So much so that Father Iparraguirre, in the edition with various 'Directories', gathers these statements from the period: 'Father Ignatius allowed two days for the foundation; to distinguish point by point and take into account the supreme importance to be given to the understanding and penetration of the foundation... In the foundation of the Exercises lies the foundation for making choices. It is a difficult matter. The foundation for making choices is indifference, because it leads to a good choice. Note that this is one of the most essential points of the Exercises.'

These words show us the crucial importance accorded by Ignatius and the first Exercise directors to the principle and foundation. We can say without any doubt that these are Exercises for making choices (that is, restructuring our life), whatever the subject of choice, since our whole life is a matter for the divine will. Because they are intended to enable us to make such choices, the Exercises cannot be regarded as merely another retreat formula. The Exercises are intended to change our life radically, affecting the large movements of our spirit through free choices. So those who are not prepared for this radical change or, as Ignatius puts it, to set aside their own wishes and interests, would be better off doing some other Christian activity rather than the Exercises.

2. *Principle and foundation: Ignatian principles with which to challenge our life. Commentary on the text of the principle and foundation [23].* (First, reread the principle and foundation very slowly, allowing it to produce a reaction in the spirit.)

The text of the principle and foundation is extraordinarily rich and subtle. Although its style may sound a bit alien to our own time and taste, it contains deep and radical 'spiritual doctrine', leading us to the furthest limits of our believing humanity. Our whole life is challenged by these five principles, which we must confront in all intellectual seriousness and moral sincerity. One thing is certain: if we are hesitant in these questions of the principle and foundation there can be no firmness in the whole structure of our Christian life either. For the principle and foundation is just that, at the basis of everything.

First principle: Do I accept that, as a human being, I am a creature, someone essentially and dynamically linked to the person of my God and Lord, to whom I owe 'praise, reverence and service'? My freedom is mediated (although never dominated) by my dependence. Do I admit this mediation in my daily life or do I prefer to set myself aside from my God and Lord? In a secular society, it is absolutely necessary to recover the sense of God, as the primary reference point for all human existence. These are the roots of our inevitable creaturehood.

Second principle: Do I accept that everything that exists has been given to me and belongs to me in order that it may help me to realise my primary condition of creaturehood? And in consequence do I put into practice the Ignatian rule of 'only... insofar as'? Am I capable of controlling my thoughts and affections with regard to other creatures? My choices are also mediated by my end. And this fact confers upon my life a permanent attention to choosing, in order to choose correctly. The opposite of this attention is spiritual superficiality and selfish evasion. We must be wary of both these possibilities that crop up so frequently.

Third principle: Do I accept that in order to be able to choose in the prescribed manner I must adopt a serene attitude of indifference, which permits me to discern what my God and Lord wants, so that I may encounter him in my use of creatures? We speak of an active indifference, meaning one that dominates my spontaneous impulses so that they do not interfere with this necessary discernment. Do I act so spontaneously that it becomes impossible for me to exercise the fundamental virtue of indifference, or have I acquired this virtue in such a way that I can easily practise spiritual discernment in my daily life?

Fourth principle: 'Only desiring and choosing...' indicates that what we have said ought to be the object of our deepest desires. What do I really want in the end? It also implies that the whole process must take place with a total capacity to choose, that is, in complete freedom. Do I freely live with my option for my God and Lord or has this option succumbed to monotony and become an obligatory and almost intolerable burden? Freedom is our greatest responsibility because it humanises or dehumanises us.

Fifth principle: '...the more...' According to the best Ignatian interpreters, this more, even here, is Jesus Christ. This 'more' will be repeated constantly throughout all the Exercises. And the reason is very simple: in Jesus Christ is the wisdom and power of the Father (1 Cor 1:17-25), where the will of God our Lord has already been revealed in history. Jesus fulfilled it completely by means of the paschal mystery, the mystery of his passion and resurrection. So much so that no one can manage to desire and choose 'the more' if they do not desire and choose as Jesus Christ desired and chose. Therefore [167], in which Ignatius comments on the 'third kind of humility' (that is, fully identifying love), is the centre and heart of all the Exercises: the fullness of what is most Christ-like. This is what Ignatius is proposing to the exerciser. We shall come to it later but it is already present here in the principle and foundation [23].

So here we step over the anthropological threshold in order to come to the Christological: the definition of the Ignatian human being mentioned in the Introduction is definitively realised by Jesus Christ, from whose Spirit we will choose the Father's will. And in this sense, properly speaking, we are not indifferent. We are always differentiated by our choice of that which identifies us more closely with Jesus Christ. So of the four examples given by Ignatius in the text of the principle and foundation [23], two (wealth-poverty, honour-dishonour) form a systematic part of a triad in which the saint will take on the personality of Jesus Christ and his disciples [98, 142, 146 and 167].

In other words, a text that may look like a philosophical text ends up as the purest Gospel: the way to live our whole life. We are children of the Father of our Lord Jesus Christ,

who has called us for ever to be intimate with him by doing
his will. His will, revealed in his only Son, brings all fulfilment. Read very slowly the introductory hymn in Ephesians,
which puts in biblical terms what is so crucial to an understanding of the fundamental Ignatian teaching, in biblical
terms. It is submission to joyful adoption and the experience
of the freedom enjoyed by this submission. This is the
principle and foundation of Christianity.

The exerciser will do well to go over these principles
many times. This is where the whole of Ignatian spirituality
and the dynamic of the Exercises is to be found. Ignatius
wanted to begin by laying a good foundation to his spiritual
structure and eschewed empty and idle words. He preferred
a substantial text, which takes us to the heart of our whole
life. These principles are difficult to tackle, perhaps because
we have lost the habit of confronting them, even though they
are at the basis of Christianity. Furthermore, they are absolutely biblical. Read them. Think about them. Apply them.

3. *A suggestive phrase of Nietzsche's*

The German philosopher wrote that 'anyone who knows
what living is for will always discover how to live'. In the
principle and foundation [23] Ignatius gives his answer.
What we live for is the joyful fulfilment of the fatherly will
of God our Lord. So how we live is by doing this will
choosing freely in accordance with the more of Jesus Christ.
At this precise moment in the Exercises, it is convenient to
inquire how we are getting on in this.

The answer may tell us the practical reason for our many
inner instabilities, our many mistakes in what we do and
especially the many voids in our life. On the other hand, the
deepest joy, which no one can take from us, comes from
how we live being fully consistent with what we are living
for. Then the whole of our life is single-minded. However, it
is easy to deceive ourselves. So we have to make a continual

effort to be sincere when we question and answer ourselves, so that spiritual illusions do not take the place of the most obvious reality. Only when we realise how we lie to ourselves will we begin to discover our truth. Think about this.

Let us also note that the fundamental tension of being human lies between our duty and our freedom. In Ignatian terms we have to live this as a tension between our service and our choices. A permanent attitude of service to the proclamation of God our Lord's kingdom will enable us permanently to choose the means desired by this same God our Lord to carry out this proclamation. Again we come to the fundamental theme of discernment, which from this viewpoint appears as submerging ourselves joyfully and hopefully in the very dynamic of the divine life. Anyone who sincerely wants to serve their God our Lord truly always ends up discovering his holy will. There is not the slightest doubt about this. The problem lies in the 'sincerely'.

Here the somewhat taboo theme of death arises. In general, through superficiality or repugnance we prefer to forget about it. Dying is the supreme moment in which service and choice become one, given that my total surrender to the divine mercy is fullness of service and fullness of choice. And therefore death must bring with it, in a mysterious but real form, the definitive discernment, which we usually call 'judgement'. Then, as in a mighty flash, we shall contemplate the whole of our life and the coherence of our 'service choices': eternity will also be coherent with them, in such a way that death is no more than the definitive crystallisation of our whole life. Life is not seen as a succession of single acts but as a dominant and totalising tendency of our being, thinking and doing. Day by day in our service and in our choices, we are preparing for the final crossing into God our Lord's arms, unless we have consciously and willfully rejected him. Thus to live in a state of anxiety about death is an atheist attitude (not recognising God's fatherhood) but to live without reference to death's definitive reality is an irresponsible attitude (disregarding the absolute crystallisation of our lives). In short, human beings are always accompanied in life by their mortality. We call the Christian courage to accept this with hope 'the sense of adoption'. The one who is waiting for us at the end of the road is our Father, who called us to life and who will lovingly welcome us in death. Then the circle of creaturehood will be closed because our relationship with God will be lost within God himself: we shall no longer properly speaking, be creatures (principle and foundation) but, like him, fullness of love. We need to think about all this in order to be joyful in our 'march towards death'.

4. *Related existential questions*

Having reached this point, we offer as especially important for reflection four questions that sum up the whole dynamism of human existence. In other words, these questions are an indirect version of the principle and foundation. Our answers to them will give us a genuine 'X-ray' of our state as believers. We need to pause over each of these four questions, in order to answer with absolute sincerity and honesty. All good discernment finds its 'conditions of possibility' in these questions and their answers.

4.1. *Am I centred in my life as a whole?*

– I am asking about the feeling of inner consistency which I feel day by day, as a result of my fundamental choice. The opposite would be a feeling of inner instability. Do I feel happiness, joy and hope because I am in my 'place just right'?

– The majority of spiritual crises come from this inner instability, from a certain lack of existential coherence, leaving us prey to any temporary passion. In order to live fully as a human being, we urgently need to take a stand on something we have chosen for ourselves. This aspect of the question is of great importance in the present, a time when people's thoughts and feelings are scattered so that we are unable to act coherently. Sometimes we cannot even explain to ourselves what we are thinking, even with the best intentions.

4.2. *What do I feel is frustrating my life?*

— Note (as it is crucial) that I ask the question about feeling. That is, I am seeking a rapid spontaneous answer to the question of what I feel is breaking up, scattering and trivialising my whole life. At this point it would be dangerous to let ourselves be carried away by intellectual subtleties, in which we can easily hide our weaknesses and key limitations: this is one of the great temptations of the 'evil spirit'.

— Returning to the previous question, we need to ask what de-centres my life in any of its fundamental aspects. What causes the bitter sense of frustration, of failure. We purposely do not formulate particular questions here: each person must answer for himself or herself. Finding the cause of the sense of failure, which paralyses the good, the love in my life, is a difficult task, because again the evil spirit will try and make me evade the truth and complicate my life. This is what causes some of the ultimate failures in spiritual life.

— The answer to this question may be painful or humiliating, precisely because by it we begin to discover the roots of our own sin. We have to take on the pain and the awareness as starting points for many things we shall be discovering and investigating in these Exercises.

4.3. *What am I afraid of in life?*

– For Ignatius something that has the most paralysing effect on Christian experience is fear (together with illusions). Fear is a sort of clogging web woven by the evil spirit around our attempt at holiness. We easily confuse fear with prudence. But real prudence is never paralysed; it walks serenely along the paths marked out by discernment.

– What fears frequently assail us, to the point of hindering our progress? What fears have we consciously done a deal with? Do we have any single overriding fear? Our God and Lord in revelation encourages us, gives us power and vigour through his unbreakable covenant. He always gives us something that goes far beyond fear (which is ultimately caused by our illusory idolatries). Paralysing fear never comes from God. God is action, dynamism, love. We should always remember that.

4.4. *What in particular do I hope for in my life?*

– This question is fundamental. The deepest dynamic of human life is hope. Without hope it is impossible to live happily. Without hope we cannot take on the burden of proclaiming the kingdom. And ask something more: What do I hope for from my own life? That is, from yourself, with all your talents, and such as you are known to be by God our Lord. What do you hope from your own choice, your own work, your own life, that is, from everything? This is the point at which to look for detailed answers. And if you cannot find them it means that something is wrong with your spiritual structure. The question is not peripheral but central.

– There is something else. When the sources of hope have completely dried up, it means our relation with God is sick. God is the God of hope (he who goes on being) who always shows the way forward to us. Often our relationship with God is strained because we are not where we should be, in all senses of the word. Thus hope dries up. Are you standing where you should be or are you mistaking your place as a person and as a believer? And one final point, although it seems to be stating the obvious: we lack hope when we have no reasons for hoping. So ask: what particular realities are making your hope fail?

– I would like to stress that we should not answer these crucial questions pessimistically with false a priori guilt. At this point, which is a key to what will follow, the important thing is to look at my situation objectively, to see what chances I have of being faithful to the principle and foundation. If you do not find anything negative in your situation, give thanks to God our Lord and ask for strength in the moment when difficulties come. But if you find obvious faults, as is often the case, realise at this point that the Exercises are there to solve the problem and redirect your life in accordance with the will of God our Lord. The point is to go through the complicated process walking in the truth, but never to fall into despair. Because – I repeat – our God is the God of hope.

5. Conclusions

As we shall do with all the propositions, we conclude by asking a series of questions summing up the material, so that each exerciser can personalise the objectives. These questions should be considered very slowly, because perhaps a large part of the result of the Exercises may be contained in them. I suggest it is convenient to answer them in writing so as to have a record of your personal spiritual experience, which will be useful for reference later.

But before we put these questions, here is one final consideration, summing up all we have said about the principle and foundation. Everything that makes up the framework of our life is created. Therefore it needs clear spiritual discernment from the viewpoint of the person of Jesus Christ as we find him in the Gospel. However painful it may be, we must radically eliminate ancestral prejudices and final answers. The Ignatian doctrine in the principle and foundation [23] shows us human life as a permanent and mysterious encounter with creatures and reality, which we must choose or reject afresh according to God's will in every case. Nothing and no one is absolute in our life. Only the infinite lordship of God our Lord, revealed in Jesus Christ through the power of the Spirit. Once again duty and freedom join hands without any difficulty. Moreover all this enables us to attain a sovereign state of inner freedom, eliminate all the false idols which are creatures, in order to serve the Lord with joy. Thus we collaborate in the liberating freedom of human history. The *principle and foundation* of our life is a clear-sighted freedom which submits in joyful service to God's wisdom, and does his holy will.

Suggestions for particular reflection

— In our daily lives do we conjugate the complementary dimensions of duty/service/motive and freedom/choice/ means? Or do we incline towards one and neglect the other, thereby creating in ourselves a real and dangerous spiritual schizophrenia?

— Have we lost the sense of God's lordship and the habit of referring to it so that we live, more or less consciously, as practical atheists?

— Do we have the habit of discerning how to use creatures in our present life, in accordance with Jesus' guidelines in the Gospel?

— Is God's will our permanent horizon or do we live in thrall to our selfishness perhaps camouflaged by existential excuses (commitment in the world) or spiritual excuses (our inner life)?

— Are we victims of prefabricated idols of any kind, however sublime, and do we forget that every static idol is an attack against God's innovating creativity?

– In a word, where do I stand at this particular moment in my life with respect to the fundamental demands of the principle and foundation? Can I now go forward as a Christian with a sure vision in spite of the pain this may cause me? Here at the beginning of the experience we must check out the 'self-image' we mentioned as something to be worked on throughout these Exercises. What we make of this image will sum up our whole life.

Appendix: *The Exercises from the viewpoint of the principle and foundation* [23]

'It may look – says Fr Fessard – as if the principle and foundation developed the necessary implications for beginning and leaves off without explaining all that has to be developed throughout the four weeks. Everything that has been explained will be summed up in the "Contemplation to attain Love"' [230-237]. From this point of view according to which everything is present in germ in the principle and foundation and brought to a conclusion in the 'Contemplation to attain love', we can trace the following schema for the Ignatian Exercises as a whole, showing their unity from beginning to end.

– We start with an original agreement or accord between God and humanity: principle and foundation.
– We discover the disagreement or discord produced by sin: 1st week.
– We produce the reagreement or concord through a difficult choosing to identify with Christ: 2nd, 3rd and 4th weeks.
– As a result we experience the joy of fullness in the permanent presence of God: 'Contemplation to attain love'.
The anthropological becomes Christological, because the resolution of the bi-polarity between transcendence and immanence, is, as we have seen, Jesus Christ, the Man-God.

The 'Contemplation to attain love' is a way of carrying out the principle and foundation through a loving identification with Christ. All creatures are contemplated and experienced from the viewpoint of Jesus Christ and thus become help, union, enjoyment of God our Lord, who continually reveals himself to me in them. It is the fullness of mystical experience, when my whole life is adapted to the divine will in its use of natural reality. There is no interruption once I have overcome my selfishness and surrendered my whole person to the person of the Father, in Jesus Christ the Son through the Spirit. We will see how such a surrender takes place in the evangelical environment of the Church, the historical Jesus Christ in human time and space. The Church lives from Mary's motherhood and daily gives birth to the Son in order to give him to us. This is our life in accordance with the Ignatian model. A model which has shaped the holiness of men and women who were fundamentally important in Christian history.

Second day:
Temptation and conversion:

Morning prayer. The three prayers of 'temptation, conversion and forgiveness'.

Proposition for the morning. 'The basic temptations in Christian life'.

Propositions for the afternoon. 'Permanent conversion as a response to the structure of temptation' and 'From sin to forgiveness'.

Both subjects should be introduced together. Their different aspects can be stressed according to the circumstances.

Prayer of temptation

Day by day I see:
like a child jostled hither and thither,
the spirit of evil plays with me.
And takes me where I do not want to go.
And twists my deepest convictions.
Aware of God as my Father
and of my freedom transcended by love,
in order to make my life a fulfilling service,
I do not want to subject myself to temptation
which lures me to 'disorderly doings',
as Ignatius would say.

I accumulate wealth possessively
which shows the falseness of my poverty.
I delight in vainglory
which resents the slightest disparagement.
I dominate others through my pride,
whereas my humility is abused.

The snares and chains of the 'spirit of evil'
imprison me
and I do not offer any bold resistance.
Because I go on believing everything depends on me.
On my impotent self will.
And I am completely mistaken.

So, Lord of victory,
my life staggers from one fall and another
and I have the distressing feeling of defeat.

Humiliated by so many
great illusions destroyed,
I pray you, Lord of victory,
to set me in you to give me strength.

Where there is wealth, give me poverty.
Where there is vain glory, give me disparagement.
Where there is pride, give me humility.

Because I yearn to repeat your life among human beings,
without subterfuge or holding back,
clasping your risen cross,
wood where all temptation is defeated,
wood of salvation.

Tempt me with love, Lord Jesus.
Tempt me heart to heart.

Prayer of conversion

Out of the depths
I cry to you, Lord:
Lord, hear my prayer.

The prayer in which I acknowledge my sin,
all the sins throughout my life.
I want to turn again completely
in order to reenter your courts
of serenity, hope and sweetness.

A prayer which recalls the psalmist's words:
Lord, give me a pure heart;
Lord, give me an upright spirit:
refine me as gold is refined in a crucible.

The time has come
when these are not mere words,
but the deepest expression of my own desire.

I am tired of going along winding roads,
tired of unhappy company,
tired of so much superficiality.

I turn my gaze towards you, God who welcomes me,
and I ask you to accept my heart's conversion
to truth, justice and freedom.

I know myself and I know I will fall again.
But at this moment... accept it as something final.

Conversion from the abuse of riches,
humiliating the poor with my squandering...
Conversion from the abuse of vainglory,
setting myself above myself...
conversion from the abuse of pride,
being arrogant to the humble...
Conversion from all the temptations
which I accept as a way of life that is far from you,
while I forgot the principle and foundation
of all life.

And you see that, moved by your lasting grace,
I take this decisive step wholeheartedly
and in full knowledge of the consequences:
to accept some ways that are not my ways,
to accept some plans that are not my plans,
but, finally,
to accept you, as a person to love,
and in you to love all my brothers and sisters.

My conversion is like that of Zacchaeus,
that of Nicodemus,
that of Mary Magdalene,
and so many other men and women
who met you
and remained captivated by you.

Because you are worth more than everything else,
and in you there is more joy
than anywhere else.
I know this in my bones
and it has made me change the course of my life:
you, your person, your company.

So I turn to you, Lord.
I surrender myself to you unconditionally.
Welcome me with merciful friendship
and open the mystery of your heart to me.

Prayer of forgiveness

The deepest human experience
is the experience of love.
It is above all others
because it is the most decisive, authentic and deep.

But within the universe of love,
Lord, comes your forgiveness
as that love which is above all other,
because you see further than anyone or anything.
The whole Bible is a song of this forgiveness.
But it reaches its peak in the parable of the prodigal son.

Now I am the prodigal son of the Gospel.
Now I am the one who has left your house.
Now I am the one who has experienced frustrations.
Now I am the one who longs for my father.
And I say I will return.
I say yes, I will go back to you.
I know how urgent the journey is
and how easy to retrace my steps,
because at its end I will meet you,
my God of forgiveness and love.

How often haven't you hugged me
when I came back to you...?
How often haven't you kissed me
when I came close to you...?
How often hasn't your tenderness flowed over me
when I fell in your arms?

Experience of God: experience of love.
In the depths of sin
I always discover the deeper depth
of a forgiveness which is love,
of a love that becomes forgiveness.

So take me in your fatherly arms,
clothe me in your grace
(which is Jesus Christ, ever alive).
And prepare the banquet of the Eucharist
so that I may eat and drink
forgiveness, salvation and love.

Now I am tired of shameful evasions,
provoked by the delirium of a pagan society.
I want to recover the experience
of your person,
your closeness,
your way of life.
I know that if you forgive me
I must forgive others too,
so as not to be rejected by you.
Unstinting forgiveness:
seventy times seven.
And with joy in my heart.

My Father who is in glory,
be to me the loving father of the prodigal son.

≈ ≈ ≈

The basic temptations in Christian life

1. The search for God's will, which we have discovered to be the absolute goal of our life, is held up by certain structural or congenital difficulties endangering us as people and as Christians. According to both the principle and foundation [23] and Mark 8:34-37 (which just speaks of 'life' without any dichotomy), the two things are the same, because the Christian's personality is a single compact entity.

So we can summarise and define these difficulties in seeking, finding and doing God's will as a temptation structure. Temptation appears as an invitation to turn away from the will of our creator and Father on the basis of certain elements arising from our own fallen nature, that is, affected by so-called 'original sin'. In this way we always carry temptation within ourselves. We can even say we live in a state of temptation. Paul has commented on all this perfectly in Romans 7:18-25.

No one therefore can boast of being free from particular temptations. We must all confront the problem as part of our unique personality.

2. In his celebrated 'Meditation on the two flags' [136-148], which he places in the second week of the Exercises but which we shall consider earlier for strictly pedagogical reasons, Ignatius deals with the theme of temptation in a vivid and original way. The saint considers human life, and even more particularly human freedom, as a battlefield in which the 'Christian structure' and the 'structure of evil' face one another. We can also describe the opponents as baptism and fallen nature, love and selfishness. These stand facing each other on the battlefield of our freedom. Their aim is to conquer our freedom and our human life as a whole.

Note that in this context Ignatius [136] speaks of sin. The Spirit of Jesus Christ (Holy Spirit) and the spirit of evil are both present from the beginning. Nothing is abstract, everything is existential and particular. The individual person is affected as a whole by personalised forces, towards whom a position must be adopted, however difficult this is. This is what John explains in his first letter (1:8-10), from the viewpoint of the 'sinner', a condition we all accept at the beginning of our daily Eucharist.

3. We can list the elements proposed by Ignatius to locate this meditation in the following order:

— The exerciser's petition [139], which is summed up in a prayer for 'knowledge' so favoured by Ignatius.
— The apostolic dimension of both Spirits [141 and 145], because it is a matter of 'tempting or inviting'.
— A vision of spiritual life as a continual choosing, and therefore in a permanent state of crisis ([135] which introduces this meditation). This brings in the need for continual 'discernment', precisely so that we can overcome the crisis by 'choosing' God's will [rules 313-336].

With these three elements, which should be matter for quiet meditation, we come to the heart of the matter: how the two Spirits behave. We are, we repeat, standing before two 'inescapable movements' of the spiritual life, which underlie all choices; we have to take sides. But to do this we need to know their respective characteristics. Let us have a look at them.

4. In [142 and 146] Ignatius analyses with subtle precision the operations of the spirit of good and the spirit of evil in a series of questions, which he judges to be crucial, through personal experience. Before looking at the way they behave, we should note these introductory points:

— In each case there is a causal co-relation of elements, so that we have a genuine progressive dialectic in the two structures. (This is an important point for understanding the dynamism of spiritual life).

– The elements of the two structures are strictly opposed to one another, forming a clear schema which is also useful for examining our spiritual dynamism.

– We should not forget that all these elements are permanent features in our whole Christian existence. They are never occasional or chance presences. So we have to take them into account day by day to discover their presence, analyse their direction and take the necessary steps.

Now here is the table of all these elements, with their fundamental characteristics, so that the exerciser can easily grasp the dynamics. Later we shall comment on this table or schema at greater length.

SPIRIT OF EVIL	SPIRIT OF GOOD
(structure of temptation)	*(Christian structure)*
1. Wealth (having)	Poverty (being held)
2. Honour (appearing)	Belittlement (being subject)
3. Pride (being able)	Humility (being possessed)

Selfishness ——————————> Jn 19:5 <—————————— Love

Now for the commentary on this schema:

4.1. *Wealth versus poverty*

By wealth we mean an obsessive preoccupation for the world of 'having' (material, spiritual, intellectual, temperamental, etc.), so that lust for possession – including possession of others, which is the gravest of the sins of wealth – dominates my whole existence and becomes its driving force. The most logical result in a person who becomes accustomed to having everything and/or wanting everything, is that he/she becomes self-sufficient, despising or under-valuing the complementarity of others and, eventually, the Lord's grace. The root of this is a deep self-sufficiency, in which we bolster ourselves up by possessions. For Ignatius this is the most fundamental temptation.

As against wealth there is poverty. By poverty we mean 'being held' in all aspects of our life, without hanging on to any areas reserved for ourselves alone. This absolute openness requires me to make myself available, consciously placing myself in the hands of others, so that they can make use of me. Anyone behaving like this admits to depending on others in all life's circumstances. They do not believe they are the centre of the universe and completely independent. The root of this spiritual poverty, which logically leads, according to circumstances, to actual poverty, is the view of life as grace. When we are poor we realise we are needy and resort to others and especially to our Lord for help. For Ignatius this is the virtue that generates all others and without which it is impossible to build a spiritual life founded on truth.

4.2. *Honour versus belittlement*

By honour we mean an obsessive preoccupation with the world of 'appearances' (social, spiritual, intellectual, institutional, etc.) which should lead to applause from others and consequently to 'vainglory'). Note that vainglory is one of the most subtle temptations because it is often based on objective facts. But we are glorying in a position that has not been gained following the Lord's will but our own ungovernable desire to appear well. In these cases spiritual discernment is absolutely necessary. All this leads to immoderate self-idolatry, making us feel we deserve all honours. We may even reach the point of thinking we are giving glory to God by accepting them. The root of this sin is self-complacency, with a strong element of narcissism. Let us not forget that in a hedonistic consumer society, honour is bound to be seen as the key to worldly success.

As against honour there is belittlement. By this we mean the humble and joyful acceptance of 'being subject'. This does not mean that I undervalue myself in the least. Because I know myself I accept this situation, which identifies me with Jesus Christ and cures me of overvaluing myself. This attitude should not be a result of false humility, but of deep truth, which makes me freely available to others, accepting that sometimes I will be appreciated less than I deserve and not making an issue out of it. When this happens it smashes the self-idol I have assiduously been erecting on a little pinnacle in my life. It is the experience of life as service instead of receiving constant praise from others, which places them at my service. So my self-complacency is destroyed. Note that in speaking of something which goes so much against our way of thinking today, we only accept belittlement through an urgent desire to imitate and identify with our Lord. Ignatius makes this very clear in [147] and repeats it in various fundamental places in the Exercises. It is not a question of spiritual masochism (as some claim) but of love (as many do not accept).

4.3. *Pride versus humility*

By pride we mean an obsessive preoccupation with the world of 'power', the primary objective of a competitive society. Power of all kinds and in any circumstances: from power over people in our everyday life, to political power by means of which I can dominate human societies. Power makes me overvalue myself and reduce others, whom I think of as my servants just because I feel powerful. Naturally this means that I do not know myself deeply, I lie to myself more or less consciously, but either way it affects what I do in practice. The root of all this is thrusting ourselves to the top of everything, to the place which God alone should occupy, as we have already seen [23]. He is my principle and foundation. Sinning through power is the most anti-evangelical sin there is, because it implies the negation of the passion and weakness of Jesus Christ, which he accepted in littleness.

As against pride, there is humility. By humility we mean a joyful inner 'being possessed' by others, in spite of which, as I walk in the truth, I am very aware of my qualities and virtues. It is a matter of accepting the truth and using it to be useful to others, without any boasting on my part and without claiming rights. My concern, once again, is to imitate and identify myself with our Lord, who was humble and completely possessed by the paschal mystery. Perhaps I will find this painful but it will certainly purify me of my selfish pride. It is a question of living in truth, knowing myself in depth and still making my whole person a splendid gift, without asking for anything in exchange. When this happens I have begun sharing the Lord's experience, begun truly to live Christianity and this brings a joy no one can take away. It is the goal of the 'process of holiness' which we should all aspire to. Thus we can live with serene intensity and carry out our purpose as creatures and children of God.

As was indicated in the schema, there is a head-on confrontation between love and selfishness. The former places God's evangelical will at the centre of my existence, whereas the latter places myself and my whims at the centre instead. Of course there can be intermediate positions, which do not opt radically for either of the two poles. But generally speaking these positions end up on the side of selfishness, as experience shows. What is the most efficacious reference point to resolve the issue? Simply, the one we indicated in the schema: quiet contemplation of Jesus Christ when Pilate shows him to the crowd and says: 'Here is the man.' This is the true man: poor, despised and humiliated but for that very reason the Father's salvation for us through the action of the Spirit. It is certain he will rise again but from an ignominious death. In this sense [147] is the key to this whole meditation. It is a discourse by Ignatius on the whole. In this paragraph we ask for poverty, belittlement and humility... 'in order to imitate him more in them'. It is a question of love, that leads us to want to be like the person we love, in the most intense and precise way possible. If you do not experience the presence of Jesus Christ in your life as 'a reference point' these choices are meaningless, because you cannot understand their root, which is love. For this reason Christianity is a 'choice of love'. We experience the tension between the spirit of good and of evil in an unceasing war on the battlefield of our will. At any rate, the exerciser is warned of the danger of asking for what is contained in [146], because... it may be granted by the Lord and it will inevitably cause complications in your life. Nevertheless, this is the way Jesus Christ went and Jesus Christ is the paradigm. From all this two suggestions arise:

– Where does my basic dynamism spring from? From the option for selfishness or for love?
– Am I beginning to relate that 'current image' mentioned in the introduction with these new data? The important thing is a detailed restructuring of my life.

We need to pause to answer these suggestions.

5. *Temptations of Jesus Christ* (Mt 4:1-11). The confrontation with the structure of selfish temptation is plainly related in the life of God made flesh. His messiahship (his own personal identity which integrates his self and his mission) comes into direct collision with the mystery of the negation of God's will throughout the three suggestions made to him by the spirit of evil. Let us recall the story of Yahweh's servant, who attains triumph through human defeat (Is 42:49). This is the fundamental problem here, which we have never wholly accepted in our lives as Christians. The salvation criteria of poverty, belittlement and humility disconcert us and scandalise us. We may shamefully flee from them, or oppose them with a stiff dose of prudence (Is 58:8-9). Nevertheless, Christian life is a risk. We have to live among the trials of the world in order to live the Gospel. In imitation of Jesus Christ who takes a risk in his temptations, but in them and through them keeps hold of his mission to serve and save, as the humble and despised Messiah.

6. *From this viewpoint being a sinner* means freely accepting the structure of evil, embodied in the fundamental

temptations we have discussed. It means subtle acts of selfishness which deny the salvation criteria mentioned above,
criteria containing the essential dynamic of God's will [23].
It is very important to acknowledge ourselves now as sinners against the Lord and his Gospel (in both the personal
and apostolic dimensions). We must also acknowledge that
we are encouraging our own personal disintegration because
we have strayed from the ultimate meaning of our life. We
can state without fear of doubt or mistake, that sin is a
radical attack against our human fullness. This is the place
for a mature understanding of hell. It is a freely accepted
situation of personal breakdown and failure as human beings, who have marginalised ourselves from the source of all
meaning, our Father and creator, and from our companions
in life, other human beings.

7. *Some consequences of what we have said*

7.1. We can almost say that the 'indifference' in the
principle and foundation [23] is eliminated, because we are
beginning to know where God's will leads, as it is manifest
in the crucified and risen Christ.

7.2. These 'critical elements' may scandalise us, but they
are fullness ('Ecce homo') and their sinful negation produces 'hell on earth': rupture with God means being left in
ultimate solitude, which the sin of selfishness always leads
to, a solitude which also affects others. This social or collective dimension of sin should never be forgotten.

7.3. As we said in our commentary on the 'structure of
evil', we have to acknowledge that we are profound sinners.
Perhaps we should be worried by a dangerous and frequent
spiritual situation. Maybe we have not left the Lord's house
but we stay in it while having done a deal with the spirit of
evil. This possible situation deserves a careful examination
of conscience to see where we stand.

7.4. At this point we need to read [63] more slowly. Here, with great subtlety Ignatius identifies the 'structure of evil' with the 'worldly structure' (in John's sense of the 'sin of the world'). And we need to ask for the three graces revealed here because they are fundamental to the right development of all spiritual life: without them we will be victims of the most elementary, even infantile illusions.

7.5. We repeat that we need to go through the conversation in [147]. We ask to live in accordance with the 'Christian structure' through the intercession of Mary, who continually prays for her children in the incarnation and the Church. Note that we are talking about grace, which we ask for in hopeful humility and not just an act of will. This is a key point: all the material in the Exercises is summed up in a repetitive series of conversations, in which Ignatius shows that 'everything is grace' from the Lord. In this particular case we need to ask to go along the road that Jesus went (the road of the Exercises), which passes through poverty, belittlement and humility. Stop here. Think carefully. Take the risk. Ask for it.

7.6. *Respect the circumstances of sin*

a. We must be honest about recognising our own sin as a daily problem. We must also decide to renounce it (however painful that may be). Be we should never stop accepting ourselves with simplicity (1 Jn 3:19, 20). This is fundamental for the maintenance of healthy relations with God, avoiding any kind of despair.

b. With the sin of others we should try to become a means of help, that is, by understanding and accepting because it is only through these that anyone will open up to God's merciful forgiveness. The parable of the prodigal son, which we commented on earlier (Lk 15:12-23) shows us the way to behave in this delicate matter. We are all prodigal sons for others, and at the same time everyone else is a prodigal son for me. The mystery of sin opens the way for the other great mystery of mercy.

7.7. From all we have said, life becomes a permanent tension between the structures of good and evil, which we must continually resolve by passing from selfishness to love, in spite of the fact that on many occasions we discover we are sinners. Living is complex, difficult and costly. Living as a Christian also implies a commitment to love, which invades everything and complicates everything. But, says Ignatius, the imitation of Jesus Christ is worth it!

Suggestions for particular reflection

— Am I aware in my daily life as a Christian of the fundamental temptations, which affect my apostolic work and my personal integrity? Or do I live in a state of naive optimism, hiding from myself anything that would oblige me to change my life?

— Have I accepted that between the 'Christian structure' and the 'worldly structure' no pact is possible, because what Jesus Christ does in his paschal mystery is to denounce the 'sin of the world'? Or do I perhaps gamble for 'apostolic interests' which may not be at all clear?

— Do I try, by means of careful 'spiritual discernment' to see to what extent poverty is required of me, and belittlement and humility, in my particular circumstances? (Pay attention to this personal detail.) Do I try to do this properly without being too soft or too hard? Or do I consider these questions to be 'spiritual sophistications' without importance in the face of daily apostolic requirements?

— And in any case, how poor, belittled and humble am I personally? Anyone who does not ask these questions has never faced the real challenge or identified with Jesus Christ in any deep way.

Permanent conversion as a response
to the structure of temptation

1. With the Ignatian view of the 'two flags' [136-143] it is clear that the believer has to live in a permanent conversion crisis, in order to pass day by day from the 'selfish structure' to the 'Christian structure'. This is a very complex process, in which pain and joy are mixed in an ineluctable dialectic. If we are not continually converted, as far as possible, we remain in sin or at least in the clutches of the powerful temptations discussed above. So the dynamic of Christian life is not occasional or haphazard. It is a state of mind which should never disappear. But we cope with all this without strain and with great hope in the Lord's power and mercy. For it is he who turns our hearts of stone into hearts of flesh. Because the rhythm of our conversion is a work of grace.

2. *Conversion in the Bible*

2.1. In the Old Testament Yahweh is continually demanding that the people should smash their idols and return to the covenant. (He never gives us up for lost. He always tries to regain us through his love). Let us contemplate three occasions, among many.

− The psalmist asks − with a mixture of hope and anguish − for inner transformation, that is, purity of heart (throughout Psalm 51 but especially in verse 12).
− At the beginning of his famous chapter 40, Isaiah compares the total restructuring of human life with the new configuration of nature to be brought about by Yahweh, with a few very vivid details (40:3-5).
− Ezekiel for his part relates the genuine covenant with the practice of justice. This is a typical Old Testament theme as is justification through justice (18:21-23).

2.2. Conversion is the *New Testament's* first requirement
(Mk 1:15). It has strong apostolic resonances, because conversion and the kingdom go together. We are converted to
Jesus Christ, in whom the Father's kingdom is manifested
paradigmatically through the power of the Spirit. The important point is that the Lord's preaching always begins with
a call to conversion, which is also called 'repentance'. This
is the initial Christian experience.

2.3. Conversion is a theme running right through the *New
Testament* in different situations and complementary ways.
It is as if it were necessary to begin with conversion in
order to have the genuine experience of the fullness of
salvation.

— It is Jesus' radical invitation to Nicodemus, with clear
baptismal resonances and the presence of the Holy Spirit,
the one who mysteriously brings it about (Jn 3:3-8).

— It is the ultimate call to the rich young man, who is
unable to take the final step on the road to conversion, which
is to leave everything and follow Jesus (Lk 18:8-30).

— Conversion works through a change of life produced
by baptism, in which we die with Jesus Christ in order also
to rise with him in the paschal mystery (Rom 6:3-11).

— Conversion is produced by the fascination exercised
by the Lord's person. This is what happened to Paul. Hence
the magnificent text in Philippians 3:7-11.

— Finally, being converted means giving your life for
the kingdom, which involves painful changes, often incom-
prehensible to spectators (Mk 8:34-37).

2.4. Jesus Christ comes into the Jewish world as an example of personal conversion. We can speak of a 'Gospel of
conversion', which leads to strange situations and stresses
the personal relationship resulting from every encounter. In
other words, Jesus Christ has come to reveal himself to us
and incorporate us in his Father's will, which is illuminated
by his person and his life. Let us recall his meetings with the

first disciples: Matthew, Nicodemus, the woman of Samaria,
Mary Magdalene, Thomas, Zacchaeus, Martha and Mary
and many others. Jesus' presence converts people to the
kingdom. This is one of the great Gospel realities.

In this way the whole Bible is a story of conversion. At
every moment God comes out to meet the human being, who
is overwhelmed to the point of breaking down the 'structure
of selfishness' and surrendering to love. At this point we
should ask ourselves about our own conversion story. Has it
happened, is it going on happening, where has it led us?
What God have I discovered through it?

3. *Conversion in the whole of our spiritual or Christian
life*. Our life of faith has two distinct and complementary
dimensions: one more cordial and inward and the other more
pragmatic and outward. We may call the former conversion
of the heart and the latter conversion in deeds. Both are
absolutely necessary and we all lean more towards one than
the other.

3.1. *Conversion of the heart* is what Jesus proposes to
Nicodemus in his intricate dialogue (Jn 3:1-21). In fact by
heart we mean conversion to three fundamental realities:
sacraments, prayer and self-denial. These are realities that
the world today tends to despise in favour of other more
visible attitudes. But without this inner foundation which
makes us spiritual people, that is, led by the Holy Spirit, any
proclamation of the kingdom is bound to fail. So we have to
recover in these deep areas, in which we are directly connected with the mystery of the love of Jesus Christ, the only
one capable of truly converting us.

3.2. *Conversion in deeds*. Zacchaeus is the prototype of
this conversion (Lk 19:1-10). Once Zacchaeus has met the
Lord personally, in a unique experience, he feels an urgent
need to restructure his life. And so Zacchaeus is converted,
without realising it himself, to justice, freedom and peace.

The Church is a Church directed towards what is outside her from what is within her, in a never ending dialectic in the lives of her members. It is her duty to become involved in the great historical realities, in which she will discover, through discerning wisdom, the signs of the times, the passage of her Lord through human time and space.

When these two dimensions are separated, then we easily fall into either exaggerated spiritualism or humanism, forgetting conversion must be both of the heart and of deeds. When this happens the heart gives Christian meaning to deeds and the deeds show the authenticity of the heart's conversion. So, once again, conversion means a 'change of life' and 'existential restructuring', which are the object of the Exercises ('to order your life'). At the end of the process the exerciser is converted and makes choices. In this way my personal conversion coincides with a collective transformation, collaborating in the fullness of history, as we read in the introductory hymn to Ephesians (1:3-19). Liberation theology comes in here. We can only understand the liberation of others if at the same time we liberate ourselves in a clear option for the poor. The Gospel is good news for the poor so they are the key to its saving reality. For any conversion is for others. Otherwise it is merely a sick spiritual self-indulgence.

4. *Some particular features of conversion*

4.1. Conversion is dynamic and existential not static and ideological. It is about changing the way we live our daily lives.

4.2. Conversion is a whole not a partial experience. We cannot keep back protected zones for our sin and selfishness.

4.3. It is a radical and not a superficial reality. It reaches the roots of our passions (wealth, vainglory, pride). It takes our whole self, not just part of it.

4.4. It is a bilateral not unilateral reality. This means we accept and desire an encounter with Jesus Christ, who converts us. We realise that we ourselves are not the protagonists. Remember the words spoken in Zacchaeus' house: 'Today salvation has entered this house.'

4.5. It is a reality which requires objectivity because it is fundamentally important to accept that we are in need of conversion, acknowledge that we really are sinners, as we confess every day at the beginning of the Eucharist. Sometimes acknowledging this can be painful, but these are the rules of the game. However, this does not mean that we should be obsessed with our sinfulness.

Ideally, all these features should be permanent and united in our lives, because they are aspects of the same reality: conversion. As in practice this is humanly impossible, except in exceptional cases, we must examine our lives and our conscience to discover where we stand in this complex matter. Other questions about our spiritual life are secondary but these five features are absolutely essential.

We should ask ourselves what areas of ourselves remain still unconverted. We should be clearly aware of our unconverted areas into which we do not let Jesus Christ enter, in case he changes our selfishness into loving and complicates things for us. These are our current idols as we cross life's desert. We must break them.

5. Conversion as an instrument of joy

All that we have said may leave us perplexed. Being converted may appear to be a task that is not only difficult but overwhelming, with serious psychological consequences.

Nothing could be further from the reality. As we see from people whose lives are changed by an encounter with the Lord, conversion produces happiness, spiritual joy and hope of glory. Through the prayers in [63] and the humble offering in [147] we approach Jesus Christ, in order to do as he did in our daily lives. So being converted means being fulfilled. It means coming out of exile to reach the promised land, which is the kingdom of God. A kingdom which we begin here on earth and which we shall see completely fulfilled in glory. There is no break between the here and now, and the future fulfilment. Merely a greater intensity in our encounter, face to face with the Lord. This is the reality.

Suggestions for reflection

— Are we in a permanent state of conversion or do we consider ourselves to be in an impeccable spiritual state?

— What individual and institutional zones do we keep closed to conversion? This goes against our baptism which called us from darkness to light.

— What are our deepest fears about conversion? What areas of constant rebellion make us defensive and keep our distance from God through fear of change?

— Finally, have we realised that our commitment to proclaim the kingdom is directly related to standing with Christ? That is, we must be permanently converted to him. Or do we fail to relate the two things and thus create a schizophrenia in our Christian life between proclaiming the kingdom and personal holiness? In the Gospel Jesus stresses this relationship and its necessity for the kingdom (Jn 15:1-7).

≈ ≈ ≈

From sin to forgiveness

1. *Introduction*

As we said, surrender to the structure of sin produces a destruction of our 'believing being' and our 'human being' (which are closely united through baptism). We also paralyse ourselves and we are unable to proclaim the kingdom because we are discouraged or may even have fallen into despair. We do not usually realise the true importance of sin in the whole context of Christian life. It can seriously damage our life without even being aware of it. So once we have got this clear and accorded sin its full importance, we come into contact with this Gospel reality that turns everything upside down: in the depths of disintegration produced by sin, we discover the integration produced by the experience of that God who is Father and forgiveness. Thus sin appears, from a Christian viewpoint, as the meeting place between the sinner and our God who forgives. That is, it is a special conversion experience.

2. *The parable of the prodigal son* (Lk 15:12-23)

The whole Gospel is a demonstration of God's infinite fatherhood, which John will later sum up as follows: 'Consider how great is the love which the Father has bestowed on us in calling us his children! For that is what we are' (1 Jn 3:1). This fatherhood is illustrated vividly in our Lord's greatest parable: the prodigal son (Lk 15:12-23). The parable fleshes out John's concise phrases to the point where we even hear our God's heartbeats. He is the God of love because he is the God of inexhaustible forgiveness.

2.1. The parable relates the four main moments in any conversion:

– we are with the Father,
– we flee from the Father,
– we return to the Father,
– we are welcomed by the Father.

The whole story stresses the prodigal son's frustration. This happens so often with a sinner who misses God the Father now so far off. Longing for God is the beginning of the return of the Lord in our lives. But only someone who loves a lot – in spite of sins – can find the source of reconverted love.

2.2. The parable proposes two fundamental processes in its story of love and reunion.

a. 'I will return' (v. 18), says the son when everything has gone wrong for him and he longingly remembers his father's house. This is the moment when he humbly accepts the grace of conversion. This grace is given to us throughout our lives. It never fails us. But do we always humbly accept this grace?

b. '... and his heart went out to him...' (v. 20). This is the best phrase Luke can find to describe the father's reaction at the return of his son. This is not a moment for a moralising sermon. The father simply feels an overwhelming and unforeseen tenderness. Our God is a God of tenderness. Do we allow him to embrace us or are we hard-hearted? We need to revise our image of God in line with this parable. Many would return to their Father's house if they felt sure he would embrace them...

2.3. *Consequences of the parable*

a. The essence of repentance is not pain in the heart, but the absolute trust placed in God's heart. I repent because I love and am loved. Such great love breeds lasting trust.

b. God is above our consciousness in the sense that his mercy exceeds our own consciousness of guilt, as is usually the case with parents and children. With this in mind we should read the text in 1 John 3:19-20 very slowly. This is a text we should always keep very much in mind in the vicissitudes of our Christian pilgrimage.

c. As we say in the Our Father (now we understand why it is the great prayer of the New Testament), if God forgives us so freely, we must do likewise to others. We should forgive others, among other reasons, because if we do not God cannot forgive us. Every Christian must be a bringer of divine forgiveness for others.

The parable of the prodigal son means an authentic revolution in Christian behaviour. For God changes complexion and really becomes the Father of our Lord Jesus Christ, as Paul says. And he involves us in practical loving, as in when we forgive people. All relationships from the most elemental interpersonal ties to international relations, will change radically, if we all consider ourselves to be children of the same Father and therefore brothers and sisters. We must apply all this to our lives, particularly in our own immediate community.

3. *Recovery of the sacrament of penance*

We must recover the sacrament of penance in all its depth in terms of what we have been saying. Ultimately, the sacrament of penance is the special place to experience the integrating fatherhood of our God, in forgiveness which completely reconciles and radically eliminates human sin. Every negative approach – on the lines of a court held by God – should be eliminated, in favour of a hopeful view of this sacrament which communicates new life in the same way as the paschal communication of baptism (Rom 6:3-5).

This takes place in two dimensions:

3.1. I must feel responsible for myself to God, against whom I have sinned.

3.2 I must feel responsible for the community to God and to the community, against whom I have also sinned.

This double aspect should show us the necessity of profound reconciliation with God and the community, asking both for forgiveness in humble sincerity. Then I will feel my God and my community looking at me with that transforming gaze Jesus rested upon Peter as he crumbled and denied – so that Peter wept bitterly (Lk 22:61-62).

In short, we should be more serious about our Christian practice and consciously recover this sacrament of reconciliation in all its breadth.

4. *The Ignatian goal*

In his meditations on sins Ignatius includes one of his most important conversations, the conversation with the crucified Christ [53]. Contemplating Jesus on the cross Ignatius understands how much the Father has loved us (1 Jn 4:9) and how much the Son loved us in his mortal life. Therefore he makes the exerciser ask himself three things:

- What have I done for Christ?
- What am I doing for Christ?
- What must I do for Christ?

So in this experience of the Exercises a circle is closed. The mystery of sin which shattered our Father and creator's [23] saving plans, is left behind. And we come face to face with the person of the Lord Jesus, as we ask ourselves about a committed future: what must I do for Christ? We know that in Jesus Christ the Father's will has been completely revealed.

I think that the best introduction to what follows in the Exercises are the words of John: 'Whoever claims to be dwelling in God must live as Christ himself lived' (1 Jn 2:6). This is the most important task in our life: to identify with Jesus Christ (in poverty, belittlement and humility) to follow Jesus Christ through love, in a daily victory over wealth, vainglory and pride. Knowing that the Lord is always with us.

Suggestions for particular reflection

— Do we live with a deep, though serene, awareness of sin, or is it something we have already set aside from our spiritual life, as we are lost in ambiguous love?

— Do we have absolute trust in God's fatherly attitude towards any sin we may commit? A sin should never modify the fundamental dynamism of an existential option in the Church. This would mean remaining in the same sin instead of a bracing re-encounter with love. Pay attention to vocational crises (of all kinds) which are motivated solely by a sinful situation. At such moments a genuine 'spiritual counsel' is important.

— Do we experience the community dimension of sin, so that we share in the sin of the world, which is in real opposition to God's saving plan?

— How do we think of the sacrament of penance and what place does it have in our lives? Has it become a mere ritual because we ignore its underlying depths, which is the greatness of complete conversion to God's love?

Third day:
The incarnation

Morning prayer. Incarnation and encounter prayers.

Proposition for the morning. 'The incarnation, revelation of the radical mystery of Jesus Christ'.

Proposition for the afternoon. 'Personal encounter with Jesus Christ, the foundation of Christian experience'.

Before the Eucharist. 'Prayer to the the Lord of our calling'.

Incarnation prayer

When the fullness of time arrived,
when the ages were ripe,
the Most Holy Trinity fulfilled its eternal plan:
'And the Word became flesh and dwelt among us.'

Even today, Lord of the incarnation,
your action surprises and overwhelms me.
There you are, taking flesh from the Virgin Mary,
which is like taking flesh from all humanity,
which is so stained by selfish sin.
There you are, tiny in a woman's womb,
the eternal one now in time,
the immeasurable now in space,
the infinite now in history.
It fills me with surprise, amazement, even... doubt:
what happened to bring about such a great miracle?

What happened is that God had always
looked upon us with loving kindness.
And he wanted to recover us.
He wanted to do it by sharing our lot.
He wanted to be a child in a woman's womb.
So the incarnation happened.
It is a loving plan,
to proclaim that love
is the instrument of salvation.

Henceforth, incarnate Lord,
history is your favourite and special place:
where human beings are, there you are too,
permanently in pain and joy,
in good times and bad,
hidden Godhead in delighted humanity.
Now human beings are not absolutely alone:
God is with us for ever.

All things have been touched by this incarnation.
And all things are bursting with the goodness within them.
And all things are hoping we will liberate them
to give grateful glory to the one who transformed them.
This is the 'universal song'
of all that is 'potentially good',
which we believers must sing.

From the Virgin Mary's womb
gushes a spring of hope, great hope:
the world may seem selfish
to saturation point,
but it hides an infinite love,
the love of one who was God and became world.
This is the only valid perspective for the Christian
who reproduces this mysterious incarnation in history.

Lady of Nazareth,
who by your humble and gracious 'yes'
allowed the greatest adventure of all to happen,
now conceive your Son Jesus in me.
So that I may enjoy him in me,
so that I may communicate him to others,
so that he may continue becoming human flesh
among the humans of my time.

Prayer of encounter

From all eternity
Jesus, Christ of my faith

you have come into my life.
In the Father's plans.
In Mary's womb.
In your permanent paschal mystery.
In the bread and wine.
In my human brothers and sisters.
In all creation, your word.

A single history of your presence
spoke that day
when your mild and powerful voice
urged me: 'Come and follow me.'
Time and space were summed up in this moment.
Called to intimacy,
to the proclamation of the Kingdom,
to serve others.
Called because I was.
Because your heart rested in mine
and loved it crazily.

Today, Lord,
Jesus, Christ of my faith,
I look into your face, disappointed and perplexed
because I know that my unconditional decision
has run into grave problems.
Understand me: I am a wavering person
who is determined to be faithful to the absolute.
Take me again,
with no concessions.
Sink my boats and break my nets.
And in the depths of my spirit
remind me of our history of love,
the history of your presence.
So that by knowing you better
I may love you more and follow you more.

≈ ≈ ≈

The incarnation as the revelation of the radical mystery of Jesus Christ

1. *Introduction.* We concluded the previous reflections with the question asked by Ignatius in the conversation with the crucified Christ [53]: 'What must I do for Christ?' Thus we introduced into the dynamics of these Exercises the person of the Lord Jesus, the way, the truth and the life for all of us. This person dominates this third part of our spiritual experience, which we have entitled 'Encounter with Jesus Christ as Lord'. Here lies the marrow of Ignatian teaching and also, of course, every Christian life.

Having reached this point we need to say something about the method of procedure. For Ignatius, the encounter with Jesus Christ becomes a 'process of identification', which will only be fulfilled in glory. Therefore in our earthly and historical life the encounter is never total because it is always in the process of being deepened. The key to this encounter and this identification process is love. We can say with Ignatius: 'allowing myself to feel affection... in order to imitate him better...' Everything in the believer's life becomes an imitation of Jesus Christ, in whom we discover our fullness as human beings. We can sum everything up thus: encountering the Lord continually in order to imitate him, in an identification process through a love which affects us deeply. This project and method are succinctly expressed in two New Testament quotations from John:

— Whoever claims to be dwelling in God must live as Christ himself lived (1 Jn 2:6)
— No one has ever seen God; God's only Son, he who is nearest to the Father's heart, has made him known (Jn 1:18).

Into this context of encounter with Jesus, with its identificatory and imitative dynamism, all the events of our life are to be set. We begin logically with the incarnation, which embraces the mystery of Birth.

2. I am inclined to place the contemplation of the incarnation and Birth [101-119] before the so-called 'Meditation on the kingdom' [91-100], in which Ignatius deals with the theme of vocation in its broadest sense. In these two great mysteries at the beginning of the Lord's life we can understand better who this Jesus Christ is who will call us or — which is the same thing – the radical essence of Jesus Christ. This is one of the major tasks of the Exercises. These two mysteries of the incarnation and Birth set up the existential environment of the Exercises which, we should not forget, are a process of identification with and imitation of Jesus Christ, Lord of life and death. So this change in the strict Ignatian order is for an obvious learning purpose, when we consider what is going on inside the exerciser. This is the reason for the change.

Before approaching these two mysteries I should like to refer to a question which is very much to the fore at the moment. It provokes heated debate and people doing the Exercises would do well to consider what they think of this question and take up a position. I am referring to so-called Christian humanism.

Christian humanism as an attitude to life is based on the theology of the incarnation: in which the divinity becomes historical and history becomes divine, two complementary realities that appear in the person of Jesus Christ, true God and true man. This means that being a Christian means being a full human being: the human and the divine agree. Furthermore the believer who consciously takes this attitude to life is bringing history to fulfilment, because he/she is drawing time and space towards the ultimate horizon, which is Jesus Christ. Paul frequently points this out (e.g., Eph 1:8-10). Thus Christian humanism is a total attitude to life. It transcends immanence and makes transcendence historical. And we should not forget that Pilate's phrase: 'Here is the man' (Jn 19:5) is fundamental for understanding everything that has been said: the poor despised humiliated man, that is, the man-saviour revealed in the suffering Christ is the true perspective. For this man will rise again and acquire a name that is above every other name (Phil 2:9).

If this is so, nobody (person or institution) can exclusively appropriate Christian humanism which belongs of its very nature to every believer, even one who does not openly acknowledge it. And if anyone (person or institution) plans one's life from this standpoint, it is not enough to say that it has 'a certain Christian inspiration'. There has to be a commitment to the whole of the Gospel as a canon for inner and outer life. This means a really careful decision, that must be meditated on deeply. This reflection is especially directed towards political entities, which claim to be Christian in inspiration but then prove fraudulent through the partiality of their interests which are not precisely Christian.

3. *Ignatius' treatment of the incarnation and birth contains features which are maintained throughout the whole of Jesus' life*. From [101 to 119] Ignatius develops some complex matters, which in their most essential aspects are those that will remain throughout the Lord's life. The exerciser will do well to read in advance all the paragraphs indicated to get a general idea of everything to follow. Note that the complexity we have mentioned arises not so much from the expressions (which are simple and hallowed) as from the theology they imply (containing deep spiritual intuitions). There are three elements that must always be taken into account:

3.1 *A mystery*. The explosion of the Father's saving plan, hidden for a long time and now revealed in the Son's incarnation [102 and 107]. This sets us at the very heart of salvation history. We lose ourselves in the divine eternity, although Ignatius states the question in anthropomorphic form. The saving fact is that God in his mysterious will decides to recover humanity, through his own initiative. He goes out freely to meet our sin. This goes further than in the parable of the prodigal son we commented on earlier. It is the Father who goes in search of us by sending Jesus Christ into human history. In doing the Exercises we should allow ourselves to be overwhelmed by the greatness of this mystery. We should feel real admiration for so much divine love. This attitude will regenerate us in our deepest personal depths.

3.2. *An attitude.* In his treatment of the incarnation and birth, Ignatius uses the term contemplation as distinct from meditation for the first time. Meditation is much more discursive, and the best definition of contemplation is in the following phrase: 'as if I were present with all possible respect and reverence' [114]. In the Ignatian dynamic it means seeing, listening, watching, so that the mystery contemplated penetrates my spirit as if by osmosis. Contemplation is a purer from of spiritual life requiring enormous simplicity and humility in order to respect and reverence the mystery, without complicating it by intellectual sophistication. I think this attitude can (and should) be maintained for all the moments in Jesus' life.

3.3. *A petition.* In the contemplation of the incarnation Ignatius offers the fundamental petition of all the Exercises, which can also be regarded as the fundamental petition of a Christian life. At the very beginning of the mysteries of the Lord's life he offers the exerciser the following with admirable clarity: 'Ask for what I want: here it means asking for inner knowledge of the Lord who became man for me, so that I may love him and follow him more' [104]. For Ignatius the triple dynamic consists in inner knowledge, neither superficial nor anecdotal, which leads to love for the person of Jesus Christ, translated into following him. All this is the same as the process of identification and imitation, merely expressed in different terms.

Note that this petition implies a very pragmatic contemplation of the Lord's actual history, because inner knowledge is based on special attention to Jesus as a 'living being' and not as a theological idea. Although he does not say so, Ignatius is drawing here on his personal experiences, based on direct dealing with the Lord himself. Finally, note that the ultimate cause of this process is very clear: 'who became man for me'. In a sense the whole Christian process can be reduced to the incarnation. It is a brief phrase but a very important one to understand Ignatius' thinking.

A *mystery*. An *attitude*. A *petition*. These three elements are present in all contemplation of the life of Jesus. We should always remain in awe of the mystery as something religious that goes beyond us in its very closeness. We should also adopt a contemplative attitude and stick firmly with the story told in the Gospels. And finally we should ask repeatedly and insistently for knowledge, love and following, so that our relationship with Jesus may become fully developed. As we said before, these two contemplations contain the essential reality of the Lord and constitute the existential environment of all the Exercises. So the exerciser will do well to chew over them and extract all the juice that Ignatius put into them.

4. *Two evangelical approaches to these two mysteries.* In the Gospel story of the life of Jesus we find two texts relating to the mysteries we are dealing with. Luke's is more narrative and John's more theological. So let us say one or two things about these texts which complement Ignatius'.

4.1. *Luke's text* (1:26-38 and 2:1-7) gives us in a simple narrative the material and spiritual features of these mysteries. Once again we glimpse the poverty, belittlement and humility characteristic of the whole of Jesus' life. It seems that Luke is trying to shock the reader of his Gospel with such elemental data, which bring out the admirable power of God's apparition in human history. In this respect Luke and

Ignatius go along the same road, in search of the exerciser's surprised acceptance. An acceptance which requires a leisurely reading of these impressive texts, especially the story of the Birth which shines in its simplicity.

4.2 *John's text* (1:1-18) is the famous prologue to his Gospel, one of the deepest texts in the New Testament. It gives us a general vision of salvation history from the viewpoint of God's incarnation in Jesus. This makes it an important theological document. I would say that John is the one who best explain Luke's narrative theologically, giving guidelines for the whole New Testament. Before we examine certain aspects and consequences of this prologue, we recommend reading it through as a whole. We should let ourselves be led where the Spirit of Jesus leads us personally:

a. What dominates the whole text is that God becomes part of the world. This is stated in the colossal phrase, on which a great part of Christian theology and spirituality depend: 'and the Word became flesh' (v. 14).

b. But immediately our attention is called to the Word's confrontation with the world's structure of sin: 'The world did not know him' (vv. 5,10,11). Here lies the dramatic strength of God made man, in the duel between the structure of grace and the structure of sin, in the blessed flesh of Jesus. Thus John is foreshadowing the paschal mystery: Christ will die through his confrontation with the structure of sin, destroying sin itself by his death and thus inaugurating the 'history as love'. Note that in this context Ignatius in his contemplation of the Birth in [116], resumes the whole of the Lord's life and also proposes the paschal mystery as the summing up of the whole Christian dynamic: '... to die on the cross...' Thus both John and Ignatius see Jesus as the spotless Lamb who saves humanity by his blood from its sin. All this lies within the mystery of the incarnation, as the main element of Christ's personality. When we are born into 'new life', it is through the mystery of death and resurrection, that is, with a paschal rhythm.

c. If the Word has become flesh everything is potentially good. This verse 14 is really revolutionary because it transforms all our possible visions of the universe. Since the divinity has become incarnate in humanity, giving rise to the mystery of Jesus as Christ and Christ as Jesus, all creation has been touched at its very root. Abundant grace has been poured into the heart of things, situations and people. Living our lives from this viewpoint means living in permanent hope. There may be human sin, negativity and guilt but in the end we discover a seam of grace, which gives us a different understanding of history. Because one day God became history.

d. Verse 14 also allows us to draw the final conclusion: If Jesus became flesh, it means that he was born from a woman. This gives rise to the Virgin Mary's role as protagonist in salvation history. Mary is the one who in giving us her Son our saviour gives definitive meaning to human history. She thereby lays the foundation of the Church to come. The Virgin deserves to be called mother of human beings, mother of history and mother of the Church. These are not just pious sayings in our devotion but important theological truths for every believer. Mary's motherhood of Jesus is the basis of a personality without peer in human development. Do we think of her like this?

The aspects and consequences of the prologue have a series of repercussions in our lives as Christians. They are as follows:

– The Christian is inescapably in the world. We must joyfully accept our full historicity, just as Jesus did. The world, however complex it may appear, is our natural habitat. We can never escape it under pain of falling into the disgraceful sin of running away. Where and from what standpoint do we see our faith, hope and love?

— The Christian also inescapably confronts the sin of the world, accepting the persecution that this may bring with it. Jesus perfectly expressed the right attitude to adopt when he asked the Father in the Last Supper: 'I do not pray you to take them out of the world, but to keep them from evil' (Jn 17:14-19). Our manner of incarnation should be to be in the world but not of it. We must not fall into evasive spiritualism or reductionist humanism. We must not run away or allow ourselves to be seduced. In other words we are in history, giving it meaning through the transcendence of the mystery of Jesus Christ. Of course this is not easy but very difficult. But we have no alternative. Do we really live with this creative tension? In what way?

— The Christian continually makes the potential goodness actual and effective that faith reveals to be existing in reality. It is up to us to discover the traces of Christ which are in everyone and everything and not act as 'prophets of doom' (John XXIII). We must be people who generate life, give light and hope. We must lay aside pessimistic visions of reality. The importance of this attitude for the Church is enormous. We must be instruments of historical revelation in the Church's life. We must help the Church to overcome its own sin, instead of being obsessed with its deficiencies.

— The Christian is essentially 'Marian'. This means Christians must allow Mary of Nazareth to give birth to Jesus in their life. Again the Virgin appears as a key person in the history of salvation. Mary's great task is to continue to raise her Son in our history and in each one of us. Are we open to this gift of Mary's?

5. *Conclusion.* Together with Ignatius, Luke and John we have approached the mystery of the incarnation and birth. We have approached the heart of Christianity. This is the viewpoint from which we should contemplate Christian humanism and from which to understand it in all its richness. Our actions day by day in history are meant to make the Lord Jesus continue to be present in this world.

Suggestions for particular reflection

— Do we have a spiritualist idea of God-Jesus (that is, above history) or a materialist one (confusing him with it) instead of thinking of him as the one who saves history from within, thereby demonstrating his radical newness?

— Have we learnt to distinguish the values of the world and the sin of the world or do we tend to confuse these two realities through the shallowness of our apostolic and ideological vision?

— Do we have the courage to assume as positive everything that is not included in the sin of the world (selfishness), even though it may conflict with our inherited attitudes? Or do we harm the proclamation of the kingdom through lack of personal and social incarnation in the Church?

— Do we accept that the dynamic schema of death-resurrection is produced by this same mystery of the incarnation? Or do we incline towards one or the other of these two elements, thus destroying the paschal reality?

— Do we notice the divinity's presence in our humanity and live as people with a profoundly Christian identity? Or do we live on the sidelines of the mystery of the incarnation?

— Do we open ourselves like Mary to the power of the Spirit, so that the incarnation can continue happening today in us? Or do we think it is something to achieve through natural means?

It would be interesting to relate John's prologue to his first letter and the discourse at the Last Supper.

≈ ≈ ≈

**Personal encounter with Jesus (calling)
as the foundation of Christian experience**

1. *Introduction*

Jesus Christ made man and born of woman, mystery of

mysteries and fullness of clarity, comes into our lives one day and calls us unequivocally but also respectfully, 'to be his companions and to be sent out to proclaim the Gospel', as we read in the account of the choosing of the twelve (Mk 3:13-19).

At this point between meditation and contemplation it is appropriate first of all graphically to recall the experience of our first calling, its original meaning for us. It was the beginning of the story of friendship and faithfulness which in adult life makes us 'believers in him and choosing him'. We should spend as long as necessary on this task of recovering the past, which has ripened into the present and which also shapes our future. We must not forget that the Lord's calling, which comes to different people in different ways is always the same in essence (cf the text quoted from Mark). But it acquires very particular characteristics in each case (talents, personality, history, etc.) and in these characteristics we must look for what is special to each calling. It would do no harm in this context to reread chapters 11 and 12 of the First Letter to the Corinthians, in which Paul sets out the dialectic between the unity of the Church and the multiplicity of gifts. What matters is to recover the vivid authenticity of our first calling. Now years later we should go back and realise – what we easily forget – that we have really been called by Jesus.

2. *The Ignatian parable of two Gospel texts*

2.1. Ignatius sets out the theme of vocation in one of his best known texts using images from his former experiences as a soldier: 'Being summoned to serve a temporal king helps us contemplate the life of the eternal King' [91-100]. Note that it is not meditation or contemplation. It is a reference point for a better understanding of a fundamental reality. It is a way of stressing its radical character as can be deduced from the concluding conversation [97 and 98].

The Ignatian key functions by comparison and accumulation: if we do what we do for a human king (if we do what we do for the sake of anything human...) how much more should we do it for the King of history, Jesus Christ (what will we not do when the invitation comes from God...). At this moment in our lives with its political, economic, professional and even religious loyalties it seems to me that the parable works admirably. Many believers cause scandal by the disproportion between their enthusiasm for temporal matters and eternal. This is something we should reflect on continually and examine our conscience.

2.2. The two Gospel texts are included because they present two different and complementary forms of calling, to be found during Jesus' life on earth. A meeting with the Lord never happens in precisely the same way. He is the God of surprises, questioning, commanding and suggesting. Or all these things at once. Sometimes he reveals himself in one way and sometimes in another.

For example, in Matthew 4:18-22, when he meets the fishermen at their daily work, Jesus reveals the radicality of the call ('Come with me'). They all come, they leave everything and set out on the new fishing trip proposed by Jesus. When the Lord calls, everything else becomes secondary. A calling is a commitment to Jesus and that is why it is the crucial moment in a believer's life.

For example, in John 1:35-42, when John the Baptist sends his own disciples to the Lord, Jesus shows them how intimate the call is ('Come and see...'). The disciples ask what Jesus is like and he responds by inviting them to share his life. When the Lord walks beside us, we transfer to a different level of life, a life of living with him and like him. The call is radical and intimate and these two factors support one another. Any following of the Lord has this dialectic and each person will stress one or the other aspect more.

Although we shall go on to explore the theme at more length, I'd like to stress at the start that the call by the Lord is irrevocable. God calls with divine assurance and insistence. Whatever happens later the call is not withdrawn. How we respond to the call is another matter. We may fail. We should be very clear about this distinction.

3. Characteristics of the encounter-calling (based on the Gospel texts and Ignatius)

3.1. *It is personal and non-transferable.* Nothing can take its place and no one can explain it to us. It is the permanent key to our vocation. It is an absolutely personal experience, in which we become committed to the man who calls us to follow him. It is the definitive experience which, of course, will mature throughout our lives. When John says 'it was about four o'clock in the afternoon' (1:39), he means this whole complex and simple fact of calling [95].

3.2. *It takes place in the midst of life.* This is something we tend to forget about. We imagine the Lord takes us out of ordinary life when he calls us. In fact the opposite is the case. He calls us at the most unexpected moment so that we understand that our vocation is in the world, to bear witness to the Gospel in a selfish world [91]. We have to be faithful to our vocation while remaining in the world but not of it, just as Jesus did the will of the Father.

3.3. *This means sharing everything with him.* The Ignatian universe [95] has extraordinary force. It enables us to understand that as disciples of the Paschal Lamb we suffer the same fate, but in his company. The phrase 'with me' is extremely important in Ignatian spirituality, because it expresses the intimate union in life and death between the caller and the called. Jesus says in Matthew's Gospel 'Come with me' (Mt 4:19) and in the Gospel of John 'Come and see' (1:39). Jesus' whole priestly prayer at the Last Supper is a prayer to the Father to look after the friends who are about to be bereaved. Jesus is very much aware that we are 'with him'. Absolute solitude in the life of genuine believers is impossible: at least (that is, at most) they will always have Jesus.

3.4. *It implies a mission of salvation*. We follow the Lord to proclaim the kingdom, as we saw at the beginning the quotation from Mark 3:13-19. But in Matthew's text this dimension is even more explicit through its metaphor expressing a change of life '... and I will make you fishers of men' [95]. A vocation never stops short with the person called. We should not give priority to an obsessional quest for personal sanctity. We are called to live a radical life proclaiming the reign of freedom, justice and peace. Holiness comes through making this proclamation, and the proclamation becomes credible if the proclaimer is living a holy life. There is no dichotomy: unity is necessary in spiritual life.

3.5. *It means being completely available*. We have to give up keeping anything to ourselves. We have to burn all our boats and remain anchored for ever to the rock that is Christ. This rock never moves however high the sea. On the question of availability Ignatius now offers the exerciser paragraphs [90, 97 and 98], and Matthew twice repeats the word 'immediately' (4:20 and 22), to indicate how the disciples responded without any reserve whatsoever.

Obviously these requirements for the encounter-calling are extremely demanding. Perhaps they cannot be undertaken by all believers in all their aspects. This is the ideal calling. But I want to stress that, within our capacity, each of us should go through these characteristics, which are the genuine conditions for an affirmative response to the Lord. As the Second Vatican Council explained, this encounter-calling, however radical it may be, affects nuns, monks, priests and laity equally. The laity must live out their calling in accordance with their own particular charisma in the Church. Calling is for all believers in Jesus.

4. *Ignatian dynamic to accept the calling*
(this is a commentary on [97 and 98])

Ignatius seldom makes such a broad and majestic composition of place as he does in these paragraphs. This is to enable the exerciser to realise the seriousness of the situation. And he does not confine it to a single dynamic. He gives several, which add up to a broad spiritual and theological whole:

    – The dynamic of 'more' and affection: in order to begin, a condition for making it possible [97];
    – dynamic of self-denial and love: another condition for making it possible;
    – dynamic of imitation: (and therefore following), reproducing the features of the 'Christly structure' (poverty, belittlement, humility) [98];
    – dynamic of grace because I can only do this task if I am chosen and welcomed [98].

So where do these dynamics lead us? To the glory of the risen Lord, but with the wounds of his passion shining. Or, more bluntly, they lead to the 'Ecce homo'. Very importantly, note that it is a matter of meeting Jesus and Jesus' ways pass through painful areas, which no believer can avoid. Only in them and from them will we reach the glory of the resurrection. Here we must go on to contemplate history with serenity and hope, knowing we have been called and have really answered 'yes'.

This whole dynamic proposed by Ignatius is extremely serious, because it is a commitment. The exerciser will do well to consider whether he or she fulfils the minimum conditions for accepting an invitation that leads along mysterious ways. There is no room for naivety here.

5. *This is the basis of a 'consecrated life'*

Briefly, from this Christian calling as we have described it, a consecrated life begins in the Church. It is a life that has taken the radical option in response to Jesus' invitation and then accepts the task of imitating him with all its consequences. The imitation of Christ is the primary element for discernment.

Note that the 'consecrated life' is a way of committing yourself to Jesus alongside many others in the Church. It is not a question of quantity but of quality: I commit myself in my life in a consistent way. This is the question. If we live like this the whole Church will breathe more freely and be more friendly.

6. *Conclusion*

In conclusion we ask three practical questions:

— Remember the experience of our first calling again but now look at what has happened between then and the present moment. How do I stand?
— Recover the importance of my particular charisma, which shapes the particular way in which I have been called. Have I measured up to my charisma?
— Ask for the grace of perspective through the other grace of a permanent encounter with Jesus. What am I basing my calling on?

I conclude by saying this matter is one of the most challenging in the whole of the Exercises. We stake everything on it. It is a good thing to walk in truth and ask Our Lady of faithfulness to help us say yes continually to her Son. And to keep saying it.

Suggestions for particular reflection

− Can I recall − and keep as a permanent acquisition energising my commitment − the moment in which I had personal experience of Jesus? A moment like that in John 1:39. This is where everything began. And everything was there in embryo.

− Is Jesus Christ the centre of my Christian experience or have I replaced him by ideologies, theologies, institutions, apostolic work, all excellent things, but only secondary because they are a consequence of the former? In this respect the importance of prayer acquires enormous relevance, as personal encounter with Jesus.

− What does Jesus ask of me as a member, maybe, of a particular organisation in the Church, where I must practise the charisma of my encounter with him by doing particular work? The personal calling is the basis of the institutional and the institutional shapes and channels the personal.

− What does Jesus ask of my institution in his permanent encounter with it, in temporal activity which continually needs reshaping? Importance of 'community discernment'.

− To what point does the experience of a Christian vocation determine my whole married life in all its dimensions? Or are these two matters that I keep side by side, perhaps through fear of possible complications?

≈ ≈ ≈

Prayer to the Lord of our calling

Lord of our calling,
who call us in an unexpected and mysterious way,
who one day broke up our plans
and sent us on a disconcerting path.

Lord of our calling,
who do not accept bits and pieces of us
and who want us wholly
because you are a jealous God...

Lord of our calling,
lover of humanity to the point where you died for it
brother of all humanity,
made flesh.

Lord of our calling,
who proclaim a hard and joyful gospel.
A gospel which is your own person,
scattered through the ways of the world.

Lord of our calling
who conquered death by dying,
who won eternal life,
which we call resurrection.

Lord of our calling,
here I am before you,
hoping you will push me,
desiring that you encourage me,
asking that you support me.
Because I have shed parts of your calling along the way,
and I feel the sadness of unfaithfulness.
Because I have surrendered to others with selfishness,
and I feel the shame of having lied.
Because I have fled often from pain,
and I feel the pain of cowardice.

Lord of our calling,
here I stand before you
to offer you the spoils of my battle,
sign of my guilty weakness
and sign of my enthusiastic bravery.

If I risked myself,
it was for you.
If I have fought,
it was for you.
If I have been conquered,
it was for you.
The excuse is not valid
but the humble confession is.

Lord of our calling,
go on being my only Lord.

Let me never sell myself to anything or anyone.
Let me never grow tired.
Let my witness always be you.
And at nightfall every day
let me feel your gaze in mine
as a powerful support to my limitation.

Lord of our calling,
here I stand before you
saying yes to you again.
Nothing else.

Fourth day:
Faith and works

Morning prayer. Look at the text on the fourth day of the Exercises and the prayers 'of the beatitudes' and 'of faith and works'.

Proposition for the morning. 'The beatitudes, a plan for living life as a genuine disciple, which leads to blessedness'.

Proposition for the afternoon. 'The dialectic between faith and works'.

The fourth day

Having reached this point it is appropriate to reflect on the material for the fourth day of the Exercises. This is a day on which we must pay close attention in order to progress in the task we set ourselves of reshaping our own image through our actions, thoughts, ambitions and desires. Unless the Ignatian Exercises enable us to transform our actual lives, they do not achieve their aim. This is not for the sake of an exaggerated practicality, but because it is in life as we actually live it that we succeed in demonstrating our theological and spiritual progression or regression. Everything else may be a fascinating montage, completely apart from the Father's will.

So this fourth day has an eminently practical character. We shall take first the beatitudes in Matthew as an indispensable reference point to test our imitation and following of Jesus. Then we sum up this whole question by reflecting on the most important dialectic between faith and works, a theme that runs right through the New Testament. We have to discover whether we have a 'Christly style' or whether our Christian life is pure speculation. Always remembering John's words: 'Whoever claims to be dwelling in him must live as Christ himself lived' (1 Jn 2:6).

Up till now we have been considering the essence of the Christian mystery (incarnation and birth) by contemplating it with reference to ourselves (calling). Now we must try to discover what is our personal reaction to this call to share in the essential Christian task, which is doing the Father's will. From the principle and foundation onwards this must be the goal of our whole life.

So for the moment we are particularly interested in a kind of existential testing of our whole Christian option. Only if we have a reliable security that we have adopted the 'Christly style' can we go on to contemplate the paschal mystery, in which this style of the Lord's attains its fullness of meaning. So this is a day of practical restructuring taking into account everything we have been discussing and going towards what we shall be commenting on later.

However, we must not fall into any kind of voluntarism. It is not a question of pretending that we are what we are not (an 'image' problem). Neither should we imagine that everything comes down to an effort made by ourselves (problem of 'Pelagianism'). Once again as poor believers we test what all this grace is and with this grace, the gift of the Father in Jesus Christ through the Spirit, we face the ascending dynamic of our option for holiness. So that we may really live as Jesus lived.

≈ ≈ ≈

Prayer of the beatitudes

As you sat on the mountain you pronounced these words which were like a New Testament decalogue.

Today, Lord Jesus,
Christ of truth, light and love,
I approach this mountain where you taught
to listen to you
and turn your words over in my heart.

I am afraid of poverty without pretence
because I do not understand the richness of your gift.

I regard suffering with suspicion,
but I do not feel the serenity of being comforted.

I am violent, I fight and quarrel,
and so can I find a worthy place on earth?
Hunger and thirst for justice make me panic;
I do not feel filled but empty.
I am hard, pitiless, intransigent,
and still want pity for myself...
Do I know genuine sincerity of heart?
So why do I complain that I cannot find God?
I am afraid of working for peace,
but I still want to be called God's child.
Nobody persecutes me for being faithful,
and so I do not feel I possess God's kingdom.
Am I persecuted, insulted and slandered for your sake?
So how can I look forward to being satisfied?

These 'happiness criteria', Lord Jesus,
are not for the beyond, as is thought;
they are for here and now, as you wished.
They are a way of living as you did.
They are Gospel criteria.
They are your person in words.

I pray you for enriched poverty.
I pray you for mourning comforted.
I pray you I may make peace on earth in order to inherit it.
I pray you for hunger and thirst for justice, so that I may
    be filled.
Let me be sincere in heart because I want to see God.
Make me work for peace so that I may be called a child
    of God.
I pray you for courage to be persecuted for my faithfulness
and thus possess the kingdom of heaven.
Let me bear insults, persecution and slanders for your sake,
so that I may have glory when I meet you.

Lord Jesus Christ, teacher on the blessed mountain,
impress these 'happiness criteria' upon me.

Let me discover the satisfaction of the risk
that is the only validly Christian attitude.
Make me stand all my life on that mountain,
however much it costs.
Let me look to you
and listen to your words,
which are words of eternal life.

Prayer of faith and works

Once more, Lord Jesus,
a believer's life
requires a delicate balance
between two complementary dimensions.
The Gospel is transparent
but also complex and dialectical.
On the one hand it requires us to have firm faith,
deep and personal,
to sustain our relationship with you.
On the other hand it insists
on the importance of works,
as a sign that our faith is not really a corpse.

We have to live both these realities
at the same time, without distancing or splitting them:
faith which sustains works,
works which justify faith.
We are continually tempted
to spiritualism or more humanism,
according to the toing and froing of our spiritual life.

You on the other hand,
believed in a Father whom you knew,
and therefore you did what the Father wanted,
which was our salvation.

There were no inconsistencies in you.
Faith and works formed a compact unity
which led you both to pray and to proclaim the kingdom.
For every believer you are the model of Christian balance,
so difficult to achieve.

Therefore, Lord Jesus,
make me a person of faith and a person of works.
Further, make me produce works born of faith,
and make me have a faith strengthened by works.
Don't let my inner life disappear
as something superfluous and unimportant.
Let my external action
increase as a sacred commitment.

Then people will find in me
a sure witness to your presence,
because I behave as you did,
consistently and faithfully,
witnessing to a robust faith day by day,
and, truly committed works,
works that are born of faith.

≈ ≈ ≈

The beatitudes: a plan for living the life of a disciple which brings happiness

1. *Introduction*

Encountering Jesus, who calls us (and continually calls each and every one of us) means agreeing to follow him [104]. We follow him with a love that identifies with him and in accordance with an evangelical or Christian plan for living, developed in the beatitudes (Mt 5:1-12). It is therefore a good idea to read them through slowly to rediscover in

depth a text we have read so often and so seldom taken into
our hearts and lives. We should read so carefully that the
text surprises and almost shocks us because it certainly
shows that the Lord's criteria are not those of the neo-pagan
society in which we live. Read. Pay attention. Surprise.
Expectation. In other words an objective and subjective
recovery of the Gospel. For there is a way of life or Christian
style which enables us to detect the genuine disciple of
Christ, without any possible pretence or spiritualist decep-
tions. Those who do not experience these criteria in their
lives must surely realise that neither has the Lord really
come into it either. Perhaps there may have been a kind of
meeting but there has been no osmosis of talent and behaviour, which is the crucial thing. For the task is always the
same: to behave as Jesus behaved in every situation in life.

Note that this 'Christly style', which reveals the genuine
disciple, is very important in a secular society, in which each
person derives the validity of his inner experience from the
style of his practical behaviour. In fact, caught up as we are
in a whirl of principles and customs, what matters (and
communicates validity) is everyday behaviour as an unmistakable sign of the inner mystery we claim to be experiencing. This is the power of witness, which so often appears, for
example, in the Acts of the Apostles. People went away
believing in the inner experience of the risen Christ because
those who proclaimed it lived in a particular way. They in
their turn lived as if they had risen again. Likewise in our
time, in which everything is bought and sold, words are not
enough. What count are deeds giving outward shape and
validity to inner experiences. In other words being like Christ
in the beatitudes is the primary way to proclaim the kingdom. Any other way is meaningless.

2. *Three key points on the beatitudes*

2.1. The text of the beatitudes means that a genuine encounter with Jesus has a marked earthly character and in-

volves us in a deep historical commitment. This means that
living the beatitudes enables us to transform history from
within, challenging it by our lives.

This commitment is completely logical because the whole
Bible is a powerful summons to 'earthly commitment'. The
kingdom of God is justice in the Old Testament, because
those justified by God are the ones who practise justice
among the people, in whom the presence of the Godhead
visibly resides. And in the New Testament Jesus Christ lives
his life in a particular history, in which he commits himself
moment by moment. Because of this commitment he dies on
the shameful cross. So according to the Bible, encountering
the Lord is encountering others, who make up history. It
means 'being for others'. There is no separation between the
Christian and his life, in which the history of salvation takes
place. Everything comes down to a strong historical commitment, which complicates life both objectively and sub-
jectively, because God's word does not coincide with the
world's word. We repeat: we must live as Jesus did.

2.2. Every authentic inner experience must flow into an
outward experience, which judges it. We must behave like
Christ in the world in order to justify having an intimate
relationship with him. But here I want to stress a complementary dimension: the Church and its institutions must do
likewise. This means that internal charismata are judged by
their external projection, that is, by how they serve our
brothers and sisters, in a historical commitment. This service must be in accordance with the spirit of the beatitudes.
Therefore the Church and its institutions must transform
themselves in accordance with the requirements of this commitment in the world. In this way it must bring to light its
inner charismata in accordance with the spirit of the beatitudes. The Church was founded to bear witness to the presence of Christ, the saviour, in human history and it will
always live in a state of tension to fulfil this witness. Put
more clearly: the reference point for the great changes in the

Church is this text of Matthew's, the highest law of Christianity because it is the quintessence of the Gospel. I think this second point opens unsuspected avenues for the Church, suggesting possibilities for intense and extensive change. And the question arises: Is the Church really changing in accordance with the criteria in the beatitudes? We should linger on this point. Not to criticise but to take careful stock of the situation.

2.3. The experience of this kind of life may cause considerable pain (confronting the structure of temptation) but this pain gives rise to deep happiness (victory over selfishness and discovery of true freedom). The aim must always be to live like Jesus, to follow his call by imitating him. For this reason, because the beatitudes are genuine 'happiness criteria', the beatitudes are a 'mysticism' rather than an 'ascesis'. In fundamental union with Jesus we live in a happy way, although it also causes us pain. Masochism, weariness, negativism, contempt for reality are all inappropriate to a Christian whose faith is lived as a form of blessedness, marriage to the Lamb. All this amounts to the daily living of the paschal mystery; the 'paschal rhythm' consists in a wise dialectic between pain and joy, a dialectic which has to resolve itself in some way and does so in the risen Christ, that is, the happy Christ.

To sum up, we can say that greater temporal commitment (which will involve some pain) leads to great spiritual happiness (because we feel identified with the Lord). Furthermore, the above mentioned three fundamental criteria of the 'Christly structure' (poverty, belittlement and humility) are blessed criteria because they are specific means to attain this experience of the happiness of the beatitudes.

So everything resolves itself into hope, a way to eternal happiness, which will be the final encounter with the Lord, when we can be with him for ever. We go through human history towards this final encounter. In faith illuminated by love we discover the supreme horizon of complete fellowship. For this fellowship, the Father's ultimate will, we must live as the Son lived, that is, with these happiness criteria we call the beatitudes.

3. *The fundamental criteria of this schema*

The nine beatitudes constitute a body of doctrine about living which cannot be divided up. They add up to all the elements necessary for a Christian life. So we ought to consider the value of each one but always in the context of the rest. Another completely different question is that each person will feel greater attraction towards one or another of them, perhaps for reasons of temperament, perhaps for other spiritual reasons.

Nevertheless, going more deeply into the text (which is also of such high literary quality), we can determine a series of criteria which acquire special relevance for all of us in the present state of the world and the Church. We could call these the 'schema's fundamental criteria', because they sum up perfectly the essence of all the others at our particular historical moment.

3.1. *Criterion of poverty* in an opulent consumer society, in which wealth is unequally divided: 'Blessed are the poor in spirit, for theirs is the kingdom of heaven.' This is the victory over different forms of 'having', renouncing a wealth that oppresses and also insults those who have not: because our wealth is their poverty. Note that Jesus speaks of 'being poor' and that means that we not only live modestly but agree to really far-reaching and difficult levels of renunciation. Do we know anything of this poverty?

3.2. *Criterion of faithfulness* in a frivolous and superficial society where everything is bought and sold without respect or love for the commitments we have: 'Blessed are those who are persecuted in the cause of justice, for theirs is the kingdom of heaven.' The Lord is telling us that being faithful to our commitments (especially the Gospel, a commitment we acquired at baptism) may lead to persecution. The world in John's sense expects us to forget our promises (because they challenge its alienating though seductive values). And when we outspokenly criticise its frivolous attitude, then it will take some form of revenge in order to get rid of us. Do we ever feel the happiness of being persecuted for our faithfulness?

3.3. *Criterion of historical commitment* in a society that is unjust at all levels: 'Blessed are they who hunger and thirst for justice, for they shall be satisfied.' I am referring to all kinds of socio-historical commitments, which at times must inevitably take an explicitly political form.*

These commitments will be verified by the making of particular choices in the face of injustice. These choices must always be liberating and in defence of human rights. They are the genuine mark of Jesus Christ incarnate in the world. They assume that every human being (even the most insignificant and despised) is an 'absolute', is divine. The struggle against injustice begins with hunger and desire for justice and then at a particular moment, when we least expect it, we find ourselves involved in actual events. Am I satisfied with my commitment to justice?

3.4. *Criterion of suffering* for proclaiming Christ's name: 'Blessed are you when men revile you and persecute you and utter all manner of evil against you falsely on my account.' This criterion sums up all the others because it goes to the root of the Christian experience: the apparently negative consequences of having encountered Jesus, who calls us

* For the recent example of the six Jesuits and two women workers murdered in the Central American University, San Salvador on 16 November 1989 because of their commitment to justice, see *Companions of Jesus* by Jon Sobrino SJ and *In Memoriam* by Jon Sobrino SJ and others (both CIIR, London 1990).

because he loves us. Anyone who accepts this encounter (we saw this when we spoke about the 'two flags') also accepts a life that is scandalous to the selfish world. So logically this world will try to push us aside or maybe eliminate us, even invoking religious reasons for doing so as in the case of Jesus. The Christian causes scandal through following the admirable and dangerous beatitudes, which actually bring us blessings in this life now. If a Christian does not cause scandal to the world, this means he has given way to wealth, vainglory and pride, the typical structure of the evil one. What do we suffer for Jesus' sake?

With the historical moment we are living in very much in mind, the exerciser is asked to consider these four 'happiness criteria' as the fundamentals of the beatitudes. *Poverty, faithfulness, commitment* and *Jesus Christ* sum up their whole message. It would be good at this point to stop and ask ourselves if we cause scandal by living in the light of the beatitudes or, on the contrary, are scandalised by them.

4. *Two final considerations*

4.1 *The beatitudes as human fulfilment*. Given that being human means 'being for others' (we are human to the extent that we give ourselves and emerge from our own private world), the beatitudes criteria develop our inmost human personality and break the dichotomy. Being a Christian means being human because in both cases fulfilment lies in being for others. This is where the fulfilment of a 'consecrated life' comes in, when it is lived as genuine self-giving to others through the basic gift of the self to Jesus. In this perspective the person living a consecrated life is at the core of human fulfilment. They know that they are collaborating in the fulfilment of human history and salvation history.

4.2 *The beatitudes, a global reference point*. If we live as Christians without going through the daily mill of the beatitudes, it means we have marginalised ourselves from the 'Christly criteria'. But if we make heavy weather of our Christian lives it also means that we have lost sight of the blessed horizon of these criteria. The dialectic between death and resurrection, pain and joy is always essential for our Christian balance. So we must live in hope from the cross. We must live as risen and causing resurrection. Because from the supreme blessedness of Calvary we shall be transforming history. This is a Gospel transformation of historical time and space. This is our greatest happiness.

The whole Gospel turns on this shining text. If we look back we will understand better where God's will leads. If we look forward we know what we are saying when we affirm that we want to behave as Jesus did. As a text for our whole life the beatitudes allow us to experience in advance the happiness of heaven. Their emphasis is increasingly on a real encounter with the real Jesus. Here there is certainly no room for deception. Am I deceiving myself?

Suggestions for particular reflection

– Do we live a rootless Christianity, shut up in our ivory tower? Or are we connected through Christ to all the temporal realities of humanity, which are my realities?

– Have I gradually built a private scheme of Christian living just for myself, which I do not expose to anyone? Or do I accept and practise the beatitudes with all their consequences?

– Have I based my happiness on these criteria, as a human being and as a believer? Or do I live a life of practical hedonism? Perhaps I make myself 'all things to all men' and am gradually being absorbed by the sin of the world.

– Do I experience every day the joy of the resurrection, so that no one can take it from me? Or do I live in a state of day to day gloom, which makes my life an anti-witness?

The dialectic between faith and works

1. *Introduction*

We ended our reflection on the beatitudes by pointing out the possibility of deceiving ourselves in our Christian life. Now we are going to look at the dialectic between faith and works (between our relation to God and relation with our brothers and sisters). This is the touchstone for whether our encounter with Jesus is genuine and not just an illusion. In other words, it is necessary to work for the kingdom (the universe of deeds) from the standpoint of a previous identification with the kingdom (the universe of faith). And vice versa, we need to identify with the kingdom (faith) in order to be able to work for the kingdom (deeds). They are two correlative and complementary dimensions, in which our consistency and sincerity as Christians are at stake. Everything we have said up till now in these exercises should be put to this test.

There are two possible reductionist mistakes in dealing with this: pietism and activism. By pietism we mean a tendency to cultivate faith to the exclusion of works, which easily leads to all kinds of spiritualism. By activism we mean a tendency to cultivate works to the detriment of faith, which easily leads to all kinds of materialism. Both these positions are inadequate and we should ask ourselves where we stand in relation to them. By temperament or through hidden choices all of us tend towards one or the other extreme.

In earlier contemplations we have been stressing the aspect of faith as encounter. Now we lay more stress on deeds, but without forgetting faith. So we shall look briefly at how the New Testament insists absolutely on faith (connection with God) and at greater length at how the New Testament also insists absolutely on works (connection with humanity). But we must always remember that these are two correlative and complementary realities, which cannot be dissociated. To do so would mean breaking the single spiritual dynamic of the human person.

2. *The New Testament requirement of faith and works*

2.1. *The New Testament insists absolutely on faith* (relation to God)

a. We fundamentally need Jesus Christ (Jn 15:1-16): we can see how from the parable of the vine and its branches. The major apostolic condition is to be connected with the person of Jesus Christ ('without me you can do nothing': v. 5). According to the best interpreters there is a strong appeal to the Eucharist in this text, which implies adhesion and nourishment. At this point in the exercises anything we can say about this will always be too little: Jesus is the alpha and omega of all Christian life. Therefore it is a matter of priority to be united with him by meeting him, identifying with him and following him. The whole of the Last Supper discourse is on this subject because the Lord insists again and again on his indissoluble union with his disciples, as an integral part of the mystery of salvation (chapters 13-17).

b. We also fundamentally need his Holy Spirit (Jn 15-17; 15:26-27; 16:12-15; 1 Cor 11 and 12). We will not spend long on this point because we say more about it when we speak about the Church. But we should remember that all the charismatic functions (of holiness) in the Church are the work of the Holy Spirit, who expresses the Father and Son's holiness in his fulfilling and sanctifying gifts. Here we only want to mention the importance of prayer, as an invocation of the divine Spirit to enter the actual course of our life. And we should not forget that Jesus also broached the theme of the Spirit at the Last Supper. The Spirit will be our advocate when the Lord ascends to glory. We should use this moment to ask ourselves: to what extent do we live in relation to the Spirit, or do we fall unawares into practical Pelagianism?

As we said earlier, we have to possess the kingdom in the person of Jesus through the work of the Spirit in order to be able to proclaim it in hope. In other words, without deep experience of God, our preaching will be empty of any valid content and we will end up speaking only about ourselves.

2.2. *The New Testament insists absolutely on works* (relation to humanity)

The whole New Testament stresses this point, which is one of the original parts of the Christian message: 'Anyone who loves God also loves their brother and sister' (1 Jn 4:21). But for the sake of clarity we shall discuss this theme by taking a text from Matthew, three very short ones from the First Letter of John and one from the Letter of James. These texts can be summed up thus: 'Anyone who does not love his brother, whom he has seen, cannot love God whom he has not seen' (1 Jn 4:20). This link between God and our fellow human beings runs right through the Bible and challenges the believer strongly. There is no escape.

a. *The parable of the judgement in Matthew* (25:31-46). The most striking thing about this parable is that the supreme criterion for salvation is effective caring for our brothers and sisters, beginning with the corporal and spiritual works of mercy. Our love must go out to meet the most elementary needs of others, from hunger to loneliness. I would say that the struggle for justice begins here and that socio-historical transformation also finds in mercy a prime means of development. An obvious danger for believers is to spend our lives talking about love but not doing anything about it. Love does not only show itself in big things. It begins with this pity that is apparently easy but difficult in practice, because it is completely within our reach. It would be interesting to question ourselves about our own caring in terms of this particular Matthew text, point by point.

b. *Love for brothers and sisters in the First Letter of John*. Throughout his Letter John gives three levels of brotherly love. Together they show love is the strongest way in which a Christian can live like Jesus.

— 2:9-11: Works (meaning works of love) have power to illuminate, to overcome darkness. In other words, anyone who performs works of illuminating love will not fall into darkness. Anyone who does not love does not understand the reality around him and does not know how to behave in terms of the Gospel. Love lights a path which leads to holiness.

— 3:10-18: In this case John identifies works with a justifying love. Doing justice (which in its turn justifies) is identified with love for our brothers and sisters. This is the primary form of justice because it is what identifies us with God's heart. John offers an example which seems to have been taken from Matthew's parable. This is to help us understand what 'love in justice' is. Further on he urges us to love for real and not just 'with words'. Certainly, anyone who does not love does not transform reality, which is so often built upon injustice.

— 4:20-21: To conclude his definition of Christian works John identifies them with truth. Someone who does works of love is not a liar but someone who does not is. He warns us: it is false to say we love God (whom we have not seen) if we do not love our brothers and sisters (whom we have seen). There is no excuse possible here. In this third point works are clearly identified with love for our brothers and sisters before anything else. Certainly, anyone who does not love does not liberate. It requires real practical commitment to free our fellows from any slavery.

St John offers a complex and difficult 'Gospel of the works of love', works that illuminate, justify, open the way to truth. The possibility of deception is always present. And there is always the danger of the great illusion of false love. Therefore in this matter we must examine ourselves meticulously, trying to discover how far our love for God becomes love for our brothers and sisters. If it does not, it means we are living in darkness.

c. *Brotherly love in the Letter of James* (2:14-26). James' style is sharp. Primitive Christianity, which may have wrongly interpreted Paul's words on salvation through faith, finds the full resolution of this serious theological problem in the Letter of James.

For James faith is valid but only when it is fertile in engendering 'works of faith'. Because if it does not 'it is a corpse'. Thus works are the test of authentic faith, the only saving faith. And note that James like John gives a practical example along the lines of Matthew's parable, so that no one can be deceived. We must not take refuge in faith and forget the needs of others. Our faith must make a real fountain of charity spring up in us.

We cannot go further into this matter. Matthew, John and James jointly give love for our brothers and sisters priority. Anyone who claims to believe in a God who has revealed himself as love for humanity is bound to become like this God, even to the point of giving his life for others. Thus the New Testament, which demands faith to connect us to God, likewise demands works to connect us to our brothers and sisters. The ideal is that love of God and love of our fellows should be closely united, so that human beings send me to God and God sends me to human beings. This is what happened in the person of Jesus, true God and true man.

3. *Practical relations between these two dialectical elements*

I want to sum up what we have said under a number of brief points, beginning with a text from James: 'You see that faith was active along with his works, and faith was completed by works' (2:23), words inspired by the behaviour of the patriarch Abraham. From this viewpoint we can say:

3.1. We must be so close to Jesus that we feel the need of loving others (faith as an impulse towards works).

3.2. We should love others so much that we feel the genuineness of our faith in them (works as a guarantee of faith).

3.3. We should accept that in the long term only deep faith sustains difficult works for Christians (faith as the support of works).

3.4. We should recognise that only genuine works reveal the mystery of faith to us (works as the way of faith).

The exerciser will do well to linger on these four points, giving a succinct practical and theological summary of the relationship between faith and works.

4. *The actual works of faith*

At this point we can ask whether there are a series of 'works of faith' especially typical of our particular historical and ecclesial moment today. At the risk of being too subjective, I shall suggest three 'works of faith' specifically related to my own moment in space and time. But each person must make their his/her list of 'works of faith'.

4.1. The struggle for justice in an unjust society. It seems that the most urgent sign of the time is the call for human and religious liberation, in many different circumstances but all equally urgent. We should serve this liberation in accordance with our individual talents but also as members of institutions with their particular talents. Certainly we must commit ourselves to the struggle for justice in a society that tramples on human rights, the divine features of the Lord in his creatures. It must be practical everyday commitment, not just grand gestures. We must offer our daily lives for the liberation of our neighbour. Knowing that this task will radically complicate our lives.

4.2. *The cohesion of our communities or groups as places to exercise our vocation in the Church, discernment and work.* Community life is often trying because we fail to think of it as a special way of developing our faith and charity, so that we can hope. Our communities should be first of all places where we can live out our vocations, where through our brothers and sisters we are continually meeting our personalised Jesus. We have a common concern and the group as such has various spiritual and apostolic possibilities, as does each individual in it. Mutual support should enable us to take on heavy tasks, with the community behind us before and afterwards, enabling us both to work and to rest. Vocation, discernment, work depend on our daily experience in the community, which also transcends itself in each individual member. I think there is a lot of mileage in this. So let's go.

4.3. *The vitality of our inner life as a permanent encounter with Jesus in theological study, prayer and self-denial.* This is the most personal dimension, but also the condition for everything that has gone before. How can we commit ourselves to justice and live well in our community if our spirituality is not deep, serious and consistent? Sometimes we ask the impossible: from God and from our fellow human beings. We must begin by dedicating ourselves to systematic study of theological works, both the classics and more recent ones, to develop solid knowledge and not be swayed by the latest theological fad. We must bring theology into private and communal prayer, because study of God's word is only fulfilled when it leads to the depths of prayer. And finally self-denial. We must serenely surrender the endless demands of our own selfishness. This is the key to any solidly spiritual construction requiring difficult re-

nunciation and sacrifice. A strong inner life requires all this
and its complexity shows how much work we still have to
do here.

In my view, these are the 'works of faith' most fitted to
our particular ecclesial and historical moment. But I stress
that each person should analyse his or her own spiritual
dynamic to see whether these are appropriate. In any case
this is a question we all have to solve if we are to be
'centred' in our lives.

5. *Ignatius' attitude to works: the 'types of people'*

The most important problem for spiritual practice is not
to do the best we can at every moment, as some voluntarists
think. What is necessary is to do what God wants us to do at
every moment, whether objectively speaking it is a bigger or
a smaller thing.

Ignatius of Loyola has a brilliant meditation which he
calls the 'three types of people' [149-157]. In it he analyses
with great wisdom the relationship between God's will and
our will. The exerciser is asked to read the first and third
type because we are going to concentrate here on the one we
find most often: the second [154].

The key to Ignatius' insight in this second type is that the
person is trying to play with God's will (more or less consciously). 'They want to decide where God comes in.' This
type is determined that in this way what they want coincides
with God's will. We should see clearly how often we use
this criterion, so that we do the works we like best, claiming
this is genuinely God's will.

At the conclusion of all this material on the dialectic
between faith and works, ask yourself what your attitude is
to the will of God. Are you determined to refuse or to do
only what God asks? As we have said many times, Ignatius
proposed Exercises for restructuring ourselves. And in order
to do so it is essential to answer this question.

Suggestions for particular reflection

– Do I test my faith every day by inquiring about my works?

– Do I ponder the quality of my works by analysing the spirit of faith in which I do them day by day?

– Do I tend towards pietism or activism? Why?

– Am I accustomed to contemplating God in others, so that good works spring from this contemplation?

– What are my particular and regular 'works of faith'? This is where my Christian identification stands. For I am what I do for others in my faith in Jesus through his Spirit. It is also convenient to pause here at length, even taking notes to try and pin down 'how I am as a Christian'.

Fifth day:
Christian love

Morning prayer. Reflection on the paschal mystery and the 'Prayer of love'.

Proposition for the whole day. 'Love as specific to the Christian as disciple of Jesus'.

At the Eucharist. Remember the Maundy Thursday liturgy.

Reflection on the paschal mystery

On love, passion, resurrection, Church and Spirit.
Suggestions.

1. In Philippians 2:5-11, passion and resurrection are the fulfilment of the incarnation, which has developed by means of the 'happiness criteria' and the relationship between faith and works:
 — The passion is the fulfilment of the temporalisation of the Word, like us in everything except sin, like us even in being dead and buried, the furthest point in human negation.
 — The resurrection is the fulfilment of the divinisation of Jesus of Nazareth, who has become Lord of heaven and history as the authentic Son of the Father/God. This condition culminates in the ascension.
 Passion and resurrection comprise the paschal mystery. We must adapt ourselves to it if we want our 'Christian experience' to develop fully.

2. But the cause of the paschal mystery and its results are also key elements of it. The obvious cause is the fact of love, as Jesus' fundamental function is to reveal the Father's love to us in his own person (1 Jn 4:7-10). There is a profound dialectic, derived from the Philippians text we quoted earlier, by which the deeper the death/sin/selfishness, the larger the love/life by which divinity emerges in humanity.
 The result of the paschal mystery is the Church of the Spirit, as a permanent gift in human history of the risen Christ (Heb 2:1-4). Pentecost is the final goal of the incarna-

tion. After returning to his glory the Son fulfils his Father's will once more and sends his own Spirit to give coherence to the primitive community and make it become a genuine Church or community of believers in the paschal mystery. In this Church of the Spirit we have become believers and apostles, as Luke relates in Acts (2:14-41), to proclaim the Gospel of Jesus Christ. We proclaim the paternal revelation of God's love, fulfilled in the person of the Word through his Spirit. In other words, we announce what the Spirit of the Father and the Son has brought to birth in us in the Church, both as individuals and collectively. Every temporal commitment is born of this spiritual mysticism. If not, it is in danger of becoming a mere horizontal humanism.

≈ ≈ ≈

Prayer of love

It was the night before you suffered.
You made it a supper of friendship
and final revelation.
And in their hearts the 'new commandment'
'that you love one another as I have loved you'.

Upon these words
the greatest revolution in history depends.
It is based on fellowship
not hatred, not revenge or weapons.

From then on
where there is love, you also are there.
From then on
where there is no love, there you are not,
even though you may appear to be.
These are words that Churchmen
ought to call to mind more often.

Words which ought to make me question my life acutely:
asking myself about my love
in particular, actual, visible everyday life.

From this paschal horizon
I discover my selfish life.
Perhaps I do not mean it to be.
Perhaps I lament it.
Perhaps I do not realise.
But deeply selfish.
Especially to others, my brothers and sisters.
but also to you, my Lord.
I discover the need to love
and I do not do it.
This is my Christian tragedy.

Therefore,
Lord of the paschal mystery, fruit of love,
teach me to love truly.
With a love that transforms society,
even though this means becoming involved.
With a love that serves to the last,
even though I may be humiliated.
With a fraternal love day by day,
even though I may have to sacrifice myself.
A love that arises from my identification with you
in silent prayer,
shining charity,
and in the shared Eucharist.
When we eat your body
and drink your blood.
The Church's sacrament of love...
which produces and communicates your own love.

So let me,
Lord of hearts and history,
draw near you,

understand you,
be ruled by you.
To be initiated into the school of Christian love.

Let me not count the cost.
Or ask for rewards.
Or regard the effort.
Love that loves without stint,
simply because you did.

And we need to behave as you did.
Let this be my daily teaching:
to love as you loved.
Let this be my final teaching:
to sleep like a child
in your loving heart.

≈ ≈ ≈

Love as specific to the Christian disciple

1. *Introduction*

1. The whole of John's first letter is a clear witness to the fact that love/charity is the central element in the encounter between God and humanity, always taking place in the person of the Son (4:7-10). This means that anyone calling themselves a 'disciple of the Lord' must understand love as what is 'specifically Christian' (4:14-16). And as we shall see in the appendix to this proposition, Ignatius also centres the Exercises on love/charity [167] as the factual expression of an unconditional surrender to Jesus Christ. Meanwhile the consecrated life acquires prophetic (historical) consistency precisely through this love/charity, which takes practical shape in the promise of virginity.

2. *Data showing the centrality of love/charity*

2.1. Jesus' specific charge is to love one another as he has loved us 'to the death...' (Jn 13:31-35 and 15:12-15). As Christians we share together with other anonymous human beings in the revolution of love, which transforms human history at its roots and enables us to be in this world without belonging to it. Faith is loving and to that extent, revolutionary. A revolution that, as we shall see in the passion, implies deep denials, because nobody loves in a selfish world without being punished.

2.2. The total explanation of the paschal mystery is that 'he loved us to the end' (Jn 13:1). We will only be capable of enduring the repeated paschal dialectics of death and resurrection if we truly love, that is, if we experience in ourselves the gratifying happiness of disinterested surrender to others. Without this love for our brothers and sisters, the believer flees from the paschal mystery and surrenders to a faith which is empty of historical credibility. This is a constant problem in the Church's service when society looks at it.

2.3. At the beginning of the celebration of his passover, Jesus shows the quality and meaning of his love 'to the death' by washing feet (Jn 13:2-17). As we said, the believer's love must serve others in self denial and sacrifice. Not forgetting that in this love as service lies true happiness (related to the 'happiness criteria'). Anyone who is not prepared to kneel down and serve, offer humble help which is never domineering or self-interested, disfigures Christian love and makes it a scandal to humanity. Our Christian apostolate must begin with love as service.

2.4. The Church is structured round love as a fundamental condition of its very existence (Jn 21). The charisma of government is love, which builds a structure of unity in diversity accepted in charity. A Church raised above other reality, however attractive it might be, would not be Christian, but a purely human invention. The Church was born to serve humanity through a love that is so strong that it bears witness to its divine origin. God reveals himself apostolically in the Church's love.

Let us recall what we said about the intimate relationship between faith and works, that Christian love is related to understanding God, to doing justice to our brothers and sisters, and to bearing witness. All this emerged from quotations from the First Letter of John, the key text on Christian love.

3. *Primacy of charity over liturgy*

Jesus Christ affirms categorically that love is more important than the liturgy (Mt 5:23-4). For how can we address the hidden God if we do not love our visible brothers and sisters? This means we urgently need a radical analysis of our daily liturgical forms, however exalted they may seem. Are they the goal of a life dedicated to love? Do we turn through them to the source of love, in order to give ourselves to others afterwards more intensely and deeply? We must be very careful not to indulge in a pseudo liturgy, that is, a false dialogue with God lacking charity as its guarantee. Any form of prayer implies practical consequences or it is not valid. Obviously these statements about prayer refer above all to the Eucharist. So what practical results do I get from the eucharistic sacrifice, in which I identify myself with Jesus Christ's paschal mystery through communion?

4. *The Eucharist, sacrament of love* (1 Cor 11:23-29)

All God's love revealed in and through Jesus Christ, by means of the Spirit, is concentrated in the efficacious sign of the Eucharist. This means Christian love cannot exist without constant participation in the Eucharist, in which we drink at the very fountainhead of Christian love. Christian practice leads to the Eucharist and the Eucharist is indispensable for right practice. (It is not easy to develop these two complementary dimensions as a single dialectical reality.)

4.1. *Sacrament of Jesus' surrender through love (bread).* The Eucharist makes our service of our brothers and sisters fruitful. We must serve one another with the same self-giving as the Lord in the bread. He commands: 'Do this in memory of me', that is, 'surrender yourselves remembering me personally', surrender yourselves as an efficacious sign that you remember me. The very sacramental structure of the Eucharist lies in giving. It is impossible for us to say that we remember Jesus Christ without giving ourselves to others. At this point each of us needs to ask ourselves many things.

4.2. *Sacrament of the blood of Jesus Christ through love (cup).* The Eucharist as the efficacious seal of the new covenant in the blood of the spotless Lamb, which implies a radical commitment among those who agree to celebrate it. They even risk shedding their own blood to develop to the full the love implicit in the pact. Again the command: 'Do this in memory of me', that is, be proclaimers in blood of this new covenant, which replaces any that went before and is always superior to any private agreements we may make in our lives. We have to be brave enough to propose to our contemporaries a pact with Jesus Christ and risk shedding our blood. There is always this practical dimension with its historical context of risk.

4.3. *Sacrament of the death of Jesus Christ through love (celebration).* Proclaiming love and death is the same as proclaiming the reign of life or the risen Church in the mystery of this death. The single paschal mystery is at the heart of this sacrament. Every death for love engenders eternal life in ourselves and others. All this is fulfilled in our common celebration: 'Every time you eat and drink' we celebrate a communal death and resurrection proclaiming Jesus Christ. Without an apostolic community the Eucharist lacks meaning, because the whole eternal and historical Christ is involved in the shared bread and wine. We cannot break it down into an individualistic thrill with a falsely spiritual flavour. This would cut us off from the body of the Church which is essentially eucharistic. We are a community in death so that we may become a community in life. We should think of communities as enablers of commitment.

4.4. *Sacrament of Jesus Christ's salvation through love (sentence)*. 'Let each one examine himself.' In the Eucharist sentence is passed on our real conversion, a necessary condition for approaching the paschal sacrament, as we increasingly personally identify with Christ. Thus we are saved by the power of the sacrament. It is not mechanistic reality but a conversion, and in this sense it produces true life. Can we examine our conscience in terms of the Eucharist and make it a daily test of how we are walking the road of conversion?

Surrender, blood, death and salvation are concentrated in the *communion*, which forms a substantial part of the banquet of believing commitment. We commune in death and life in the bread and wine, to surrender ourselves to love through love and be saved from all selfishness.

We must revise the celebration of our Eucharist. Do we celebrate it in memory/in the presence of Jesus Christ or as one more liturgical rite, perhaps lacking in love for our brothers and sisters, which deprives the celebration of any profound meaning? Let us not forget that as well as 'the Church making the Eucharist' it is also true that 'the Eucharist makes the Church'. Thus both realities are complementary in relation to the body of Jesus Christ.

5. *Two appendices*

5.1. In the Exercises Ignatius confirms everything we have said about love, placing at the centre and peak of our identification with Jesus the 'three forms of humility' (and by humility he means love) [167]. This theme picks up other key themes in the Exercises [53, 98, 147] from the viewpoint of [104]. We have to love him so much and so freely that our whole life is governed only by the dynamism of his love, even though this may seem like madness ('to imitate and become more like Christ our Lord'). This is our model for living. In accordance with this we have to make all our choices (as we said when we were commenting on the 'more' in the principle and foundation), however much they may cost. Perhaps [167] is the deepest point in all the Exercises. This means that anything that does not come this way is not on the road that Ignatius thinks of as the Gospel: the road which is a progressive never ending transformation in Christ. Each of us knows our own ways very well.

5.2. This is the context in which to set virginity. It is not something merely pragmatic but the fulfilment of this absolute surrender to Jesus Christ. For love of him it does not marry anybody or anything else (giving up not just sex but also wealth, honour, power, and all the elements of the world's sin). A virginal surrender brings with it the proclamation of the kingdom, that is, of the loved person, with great passion. There can be no true virginity without an apostolic spirit.

Finally and as well as everything we have said, we can say that all Christian reality must pass through the crucible of love, to test its authenticity. Without practical love there is no Christianity. This is the great challenge for the Church in a society that rightly observes and criticises her. But let us not forget that the Church is each one of us.

Suggestions for particular reflection

– Am I clear – and does it show in my life – that the love of Jesus is the paradigm for my whole Christian life? Or have I replaced it with other realities, perhaps urgent, attractive, of the moment, but inevitably secondary, which ultimately will not sustain me as a believer?

– Do we revolutionise our society through love, which is the most original and powerful instrument of revolution? Or have we replaced it with non-evangelical weapons?

– Do we love in such a way that we are capable of experiencing Christ's paschal mystery, without giving up at the slightest difficulty? Or have we renounced any Christian activity which involves crucifixion?

– Can our love be judged objectively by our actual service day by day? Or is it just feeling and talk?

– Do I establish ecclesial and institutional relationships based on the power of love? Or do I indulge in dangerous habits, dominated by my selfishness?

– Do I live the Eucharist as a sacrament which incites me to sacrificial and community love? Or are my Eucharists mere rituals without any implications of service?

– Is my liturgy the living expression of fervent love or does it consist in empty and ritualistic actions?

– Am I clear about the world of virginity? Or have I masked it with temporal reality to which I have linked my life beyond my radical commitment to the person of the Lord Jesus?

– Do I make my marriage a life of active love, which spreads to my children and the people around me? Do I do this through a frequent committed sharing in the Eucharist?

Sixth day:
Mystery of Christ's Passion

Morning prayer. 'Prayer of the passion'.

Proposition for the whole day. 'The mystery of Jesus Christ as passion. The paschal mystery as death'.

At the Eucharist. Think of the Good Friday liturgy.

Prayer of the passion

When I contemplate you,
Lord of the wood of witness and tomb of light,
I discern in my torpid darkness
your paschal rhythm:
in the fullness of death
the most joyful life explodes.

So, paschal Lord,
you know that what I easily discern
I neither practise nor take on.
With uncontrolled passion,
with my atrocious and giddy selfishness,
I burn on the hearth of my cowardice
all the crosses and tombs
that come my way.

And then absurdly
I want to experience the joy of resurrection.
And there is no joy, Lord.
Only the cruel sense of emptiness
for one who replaced everything by nothing.

This is my rhythm, Lord.
Not a paschal rhythm but a torpid deceitful one,
overwhelmed by vain frivolity.

Today, trustful as a child,
I want to retrace your footsteps on your holy way:

drag my flesh up onto the wood of witness
and pierce my panic in the tomb of light.
To learn the paschal mystery.
An apprenticeship in experience and wisdom
in close contact with you,
beyond my cringing fear and pain,
my odious frivolity,
my appalling selfishness.

Because we never understand
the cross and the resurrection:
we live them in you
and with you, in life.

≈ ≈ ≈

The mystery of Jesus Christ as passion
The paschal mystery as death

1. *Introduction to the theme of the passion*

1.1 *The attitude of Ignatius.* When Ignatius comes to the paschal mysteries, he makes the exerciser concentrate his or her attention absolutely on the person of Jesus Christ, in order to reach the peak of identification and thereby experience the objective consequences of following him. (This has been developed throughout the contemplations on the 'public life' and clinched by the choices, during the second week.) Ignatius proposes:

– Adopting a contemplative attitude [114].

– Allowing myself to be 'affected' by all that happens to the Lord [203]. It is helpful here to contemplate Isaiah 53 (the fourth song of Yahweh's Servant), which describes the total annihilation of the Lord. Nevertheless our contemplation must be open to the mystery of glory, as all Christian passion is always penetrated by a dialectic of hope.

An excellent way of spending a day will be to take the passion as a whole, going over it with Ignatius and allowing the suffering Christ to come into my life till he transforms it in an apprenticeship to the mystery of the paschal suffering.

1.2. *Problems*

a. The passion is one of the fulfilments of the incarnation, because death is the fulfilment of the Word's entering time and becoming like us in all things except sin. We are touching the very depths of the person of Jesus Christ, which consists of a tension between humanity and divinity. It is useful here to return to John's two prologues, in his Gospel and his First Letter. In these he treats the problem from two different perspectives: in his Gospel with respect to God's total plan and in his Letter with respect to us as individuals.

b. Isn't Christ crucified a scandal? And doesn't this also apply to its role as a model? Remember the harsh warnings at Emmaus (Lk 24:13-35) and Paul's reminder to the Galatians (3:1). We find the answer to our question in the Father's 'wise madness' described by Paul in 1 Corinthians 1:18-25. Beware: we are not talking about a theoretical scandal (because intellectually we may accept it all). It is a practical scandal, that is, a scandal affecting our everyday lives, which we have to live in accordance with the dynamic of the passion. Are we affected by the passion, with its painful features and its radical confrontation? Or are we just passion intellectuals, who do not become involved with its loving suffering?

c. In the face of possible scandal Paul, in Galatians 6:14, describes the cross as the glory of the believer. It is the negation of the sin of the world, with its resulting pain and new dawn. This is an experience of faith in the passion (I believe in the mystery of the cross), in hope (the cross opens new horizons for me) and love (without it there could never be death to the sin of worldly selfishness).

1.3. The root of the mystery of the passion. We have to discover the reason for Jesus' passion, so that we do not make mistakes in our following and identification. Jesus does not die through the Father's will, as it sometimes seems to be said. It would be a human and theological absurdity to say that the Father wants the death of his only Son and would also lead us into dangerous determinism. Jesus dies (and this is implicit from the beginning of his public life) because it is consistent with the Father's will, who demands it from him as an absolute manifestation of love, as a way of living and co-existing in a world dominated by the sin of selfishness. Victory over selfishness is through the apparent defeat of love. This is the heart of the difficulty when we imitate Jesus' behaviour. We panic at the defeat and then we doubt love's historical efficacy. But if we are manifesters of love, we are suffering the same fate as our only Lord.

All this leads to a very realistic rereading of Jesus' passion story. Here are Pilate, the Pharisees, Herod, the crowd, the fleeing disciples etc., who explain all the events as sin's refusal to open itself to grace. We should avoid pietist readings that conceal the genuine problem. We should engage in deep realism, knowing that the same thing could happen to us today. And it is a fact that it is happening all over the world.

1.4. *Earlier reference points in the Exercises:*

a. Go back to [53] to take up the dialogue with the crucified Christ with more awareness. We should allow ourselves to be challenged by Ignatius' question, which presents us with an 'action crisis'.

b. Go back to [167] to contemplate how the permanent triptych of poverty, belittlement and humiliation becomes cross, death and burial, that is, absolute annihilation. Does our love for Jesus go as far as this Ignatian length? Are we willing to imitate to this point of total identification? Or have we escaped the 'mortal place'?

Pontius Pilate sums up all these considerations when he shows us the real man: 'Here is the man' (Jn 19:5). This is what Jesus is like. Not anything else. To the point where he can say: 'it is done' (Jn 19:30). Do we accept this Christ structure which we saw confronting the structure of sin (proposition 2) in open and decisive combat? What is the image of 'the man', the human that works for us in a hedon-istic consumer society? Has it got anything to do with this 'man of the passion for love'?

1.5. *Appendix.* The truth is that with this introduction we can approach Jesus' passion without needing any other ma-terial, because the great questions are set out here. But to help us even more in our contemplation of the passion, I now suggest we consider the 'passions of the passion' in an attempt to enter into Jesus' feelings during those moments which become constants in our spiritual life (Gethsemane, cross and tomb). Note however that these moments lack meaning unless we consider them in the light of what we have already said. What we have to do is to become ab-sorbed in the passion, be with the Lord and learn from the Lord.

2. *The passions of the passion*

We have said there are moments in the passion which, together with other moments, structure our whole spiritual life. These moments (Gethsemane, cross and tomb) are two-fold: they are moments of purification and also hopeful realities. Let us consider them slowly without theorising or intellectualising evasions.

2.1. *The purification of the passion.* There are situations that scrub and wring our lives ridding it of all that is selfish and sinful, so that it is totally purified. These situations occur in daily life.

a. *Gethsemane: purification of despair* (Lk 22:39-46). When his Father and friends abandon him, Jesus falls into despair, which paradoxically forces him to place everything in his Father's hands. This is the purification of all human support and also all divine intervention. To recover it in naked despair (as Tillich says). When everything fails for us and others abandon us, in everyday life, in this total solitude we have to reencounter the true God, who always gives us a fatherly welcome.

b. *Cross: purification of defeat* (Mk 15:34). Jesus cries out at the breakdown of his plans and the victory of his enemies. In this cry he feels he is forsaken by his Father. From the cross he contemplates the overwhelming and disheartening reality. His messiahship is purified of all triumphalism, in order to become a reconnection with the Father's love. The nails nail him to this love alone. Do we accept the purification of our defeats, including when we have loved to the limit?

c. *Tomb: purification of being forgotten* (Mt 15:42-7). This is the most painful of purifications. There comes a moment in which everything seems to have come to nothing and everyone 'passes you by'. This is like the tomb. Being dead and buried. Without this experience of the tomb the purification of all traces of selfishness is not complete. We should note how we flee from all tombs, all radical humiliation, being forgotten by others, in order constantly to push ourselves idolatrously.

These are the three great purifications of our spiritual life, when real difficulties arise in confronting the sin of the world: despair, defeat, being forgotten. The others always allow us escapes and excuses. But our Gethsemanes, crosses and tombs do not.

In these circumstances we should do two things:

– contemplate Jesus Christ, just that: there is love!

– identify with Jesus Christ, just that: that is the way we should go!

But on the horizon there always stands a sustaining faith in the resurrection. However we should not forget that while we are going through these purifications this faith in the resurrection does not make them any less painful. It is essential for the believer to undergo this dialectic.

Christ is the supreme anarchist because he denies that power sets the agenda and puts love in its place. Victory over the wrong values of the world must be by way of the purifications of love in the passion [63].

2.2. *The hopes of the passion*. These are the same situations as before, but contemplated as givers of hope, in so far as they are freely and consciously accepted. From the depths of the painful passion arises the joy of the hopeful passion.

a. *Gethsemane: hope in God's will* (Lk 22:39-46). Jesus reacts strongly in the garden. In a generous act of faith and hope he trusts the Father's mysterious plans (which human beings do not know) and he realises that although he has been forsaken by his friends, he still has the hidden presence of the Father. Everything is grace, that is, everything is fatherhood. And we are carried where we go in the obscure company of one who loves us to the full. Hoping in God is the most Christian act we can do, because it means recognising that a Father like ours can never fail us, however painful the circumstances. Are we men and women of hope?

b. *Cross: the hope of victory in defeat* (Lk 23:46). Love is stronger than death in defeat. It achieves the most sensational victory precisely when we seem to be most frustrated. Jesus Christ, apparently defeated, ends up committing himself into the hands of the omnipotent God, the guarantee of his loving revelation in the world. At that disastrous moment this was an act of hope. Do we place ourselves in the Father's hands when they crucify us or do we prefer to endure the crosses in our life with mere stoicism rather than as believers.

c. *Tomb: the hope of resurrection* (Mk 15:42-47). The great mystics understand this hope perfectly. Everything acquires saving meaning in the annihilation of the tomb. As the Lord says in Mark 8 the Christian has to lose his life in order to gain it. The resurrection ripens in the tomb. In the fullness of humiliation grows the victory over selfishness. These are really revolutionary criteria which may upset our everyday values. Do we hope to rise from our tombs or do we feel ourselves finally buried?

These are the three great hopes for our spiritual life, when genuine difficulties arise, which appear to wreck everything and allow the sin of the world to conquer: the Father's will, victory in defeat, resurrection from the tomb. These hopes never fail. Other more human hopes may. In these circumstances we should do two things:

– contemplate Jesus, just that: this is how power saves!
– identify with Jesus, just that: this is how we will be saved!

Even when we feel despair and abandonment, everything is channelled towards the risen Christ, our ultimate hope.

Christ is the supreme anarchist: his denial of power, which purifies him in pain, brings about the victory of love which is stronger than any human power. Love transforms all values: impotence becomes power through Christian hope. This is a difficult but necessary conviction.

3. *Conclusion*

3.1. The madness of the cross for Paul is the response to the hymn in Philippians (1 Cor 1:18-25).

3.2. Everything is worth less than Jesus Christ (Phil 3:7-11).

3.3. We have a God who understands. He has endured all our weaknesses, except sin (Heb 4:15-16).

The passion is the moment of ultimate conversion to the person of Jesus Christ, because it reveals to what point God became human. Thus it is the foundation of our hope. Everything we have said before leads to this conclusion: we must stand and struggle (really and actually) together with human beings suffering passions. This and this alone will be the sign that we stand with our crucified Lord in our own particular historical moment. Any other way of looking at the passion which ignores this summary conclusion is an evasion, that is, a lie.

Suggestions for particular reflection

— Am I inwardly affected by Jesus' passion, as something that affects me personally. Or have I turned into an object of merely intellectual or pious reflection, divorced from daily life?

— Do I accept the Father's wise madness, more powerful than human wisdom? Or have I allowed human criteria progressively to take over in my life as a Christian?

— Do I fully realise that victory over selfishness is through love's apparent defeat, however hard and paradoxical this may be? Or do I refuse to endure the 'circumstances of defeat' which occur in daily life?

— What is my image of the true man or woman? One who has suffered and risen again or a sugary Christ who knows nothing of pain and is empty of all paschal content?

— Do I allow the purifications of the passion to enter my life (despair, defeat, being forgotten)? Or do I try to purify myself by means of evasively ritual remedies, which I myself invent in order to avoid facing the mystery of annihilation?

— Do I confront the difficulties of life with the hopes of the passion (Father's will, victory in defeat and resurrection from the tomb)? Or have I created artificial sources of hope, apart from the paschal mystery?

— Do I struggle and co-suffer, because I stand with those who are suffering Christ's passion in my historical moment? Or do I avoid all painful circumstances as too much commitment and risk? Do I remain instead under the protection or on the side of the powerful of this world?

Seventh day:
Resurrection and ascension

Morning prayer. 'Resurrection prayer'.

Proposition for the morning. 'The mystery of Jesus Christ as resurrection. The passover as life'.

Proposition for the afternoon. 'The ascension: the passover as glory. Heaven'.

At the Eucharist. Think of the Easter Vigil liturgy.

Resurrection prayer

The passover of the believer,
my own passover,
does not finish in the crucified body
buried in the tomb.
The believer's passover
attains its fulfilment in the glorious body
which breaks out of the tomb
and is open to unshakable hope.

Death, where is your victory?
In the shining wounds of the crucified one,
wounds now risen from the dead,
the eternal inheritance of the Father's children
and brothers and sisters of the one who was condemned.
Christ dead and buried,
love to the extreme,
is the risen and triumphant Christ,
the fullness of divinity.

The dynamism of faith
cannot remain stuck in death and burial:
either we experience the joy of resurrection
or we have ruined our whole life,
lost its fulfilment.
We die to live.
We surrender ourselves in order to be satisfied.
We empty ourselves in order to enjoy fullness.
Furthermore, it is on the cross,

from the solitude of the tomb,
that the spring of glory rises.
We human beings, Lord, are very little.
We risk suffering and then...
then we do not know how to overcome our dismay.
Teach me the wisdom of the cross,
which is the wisdom of resurrection.
Show me the risen one in the crucified,
which is the fundamental discovery.
Reveal the beauty of your risen Son
before my eyes, which have so often been sorrowful.

Because I want to go through the world,
through life, among people
as an 'instrument of resurrection'.
I want to bring life where there is death.
To raise hope where there is despair.
Find good where nearly everybody sees only evil.
To encourage, soothe, strengthen,
instead of depressing people even more.
Let me feel myself risen
to proclaim the resurrection to all people.

Then the whole passover will have 'passed over' me.
With no short cuts. No evasions.
And my whole life will be a canticle of glory
about this magnificent reality.
From the cross and the tomb
I go towards the Father's house,
where you are waiting for me,
risen Lord.

≈ ≈ ≈

The mystery of Jesus Christ as resurrection
The paschal mystery as life

1. *Introduction to the theme of resurrection*

1.1. *The resurrection, goal of the Exercises*

The resurrection is the peak, the goal of all Christian experience and all the Exercises, because it means the final discovery of the Father's will for us, his children: that we should form the big universal family of those saved by the Messiah (Eph 1:3-14). This inaugurates a unity with Christ at the centre as a sign of ultimate fulfilment. So this call to cosmic brotherhood and sisterhood (in an eschatological vision of creation and history) arises as a categorical imperative of the Christian fact of resurrection. This is a global horizon that sometimes escapes us. It finds its most luminous expression in the Lord's prayer at the Last Supper (Jn 17:20-23).

1.2. *The resurrection as something we experience*

This 'christening', the fulfilment of our daily encounter and following of Christ, is something we experience. The risen Christ calls us by name, as he did Mary, and like Thomas we recognise him as Lord, the definitive conqueror of death. We gain access to a different life, which we call grace (sharing in the glorious life of Jesus Christ).

This encounter takes different forms in the Gospel, human forms which arise out of everyday difficulties:

- encounter following uncertainty by Mary (Jn 20:16);
- encounter following doubt by Thomas (Jn 20:28);
- encounter following despair on the road to Emmaus (Lk 24:13-35).

Out of what current perhaps painful experience do I encounter the risen Christ, in such a way that I can perceive and adopt the Lord's full will for me? Who am I at this moment of my life in relation to Jesus' resurrection?

1.3. *Ignatius' point of view*

Ignatius does not spend long on this subject, but he offers a number of points which are extraordinarily fruitful for the whole of our spiritual life:

a. *Marian context* [218-220]: Only when the Son reaches his fulfilment does Ignatius propose his Mother as someone fundamental, as the logical first receiver of the presence of her victorious Son. (This is a 'pious' but certain way of affirming Mary's sharing in the grace of the risen Christ, the source of all gifts). The theme of co-redemption is succeeded by the theme of co-salvation (identification in glory).

b. *Contemplative attitude* [218 versus 114]. Now more than ever, it is appropriate to make the mystery present to ourselves, with a simple and total self-surrender, leaving aside all other reflections of a more meditative character. We must learn to fill ourselves osmotically with this Jesus who has conquered death. He offers us the mystery of an eternal life through sharing in his own risen person. This is contemplation.

c. *Allowing ourselves to be affected by the Lord's joy* [221]. This is the same theory as in the passion, which fills our previous contemplative attitude with meaning. We should forget ourselves and our problems and become submerged in the joyful glory of the risen Christ who has appeared. Thus we share personally in his glory. Without being sentimental, here I see a possible solution to many moments of depression that threaten to overwhelm us in our daily lives. We should get into contact with Jesus Christ's expansive joy.

d. *The triumph of divinity* [223]. Ignatius is aware of what we have already called the 'fulfilment of the incarnation'. The resurrection is the fulfilment of the divinisation of Jesus of Nazareth, which began in Mary's womb. Now he has become Lord of heaven and earth. God triumphs over his enemies, especially death and sin, showing his omnipotent divine nature in the mortal/immortal flesh of his Son Jesus Christ. There is a veiled allusion to Isaiah because here too the Suffering Servant is the one who also experiences triumph.

e. *Jesus, the great comforter* [224]. For Ignatius, taking his inspiration from all the appearances in the Gospels, the fundamental task of the risen friend is to act as comforter. Thus the resurrection becomes a dynamic in our spiritual life because Jesus Christ is constantly coming out to comfort us. We all need this comfort so much in spite of pretending to others we are so strong. We should ask ourselves, is Jesus Christ, the risen Lord, our fundamental and primary comfort? What other comforts do we seek instead? We are not trying to deny the importance of human comfort, but to put everything in its place as believers.

1.4. *The paschal mystery transforms* (Phil 2:5-11)

Now we should turn back and contemplate the paschal rhythm, so well analysed by Paul in Philippians. This is how it goes: the state of love, which confronts the sin of a selfish world leads us to a cross, which raises us to life again through its very self-denial, because surrender to others transforms us. And in its turn the experience of rising gives us the courage to go on committing ourselves to love as a way of life, because we know in advance it will triumph. Thus the cross finds its true meaning in the resurrection.

If we find we are satisfied with these introductory elements (especially with the Gospel data and Ignatius' suggestions), we can stop here during our prayer, without bothering to go on any further. Remember the advice in Annotation 2.

2. *The practical dimension of the risen Christ*

The resurrection affects our human lives in such a way that it means a passage from a natural anthropology to a Christian anthropology (the baptismal anthropology, which sets us on the road to becoming 'new creatures'). We shall look at this in a series of different and complementary points, which develop the powers of the risen Christ in the practical matters of our daily lives. This and this alone is the question: Does the risen Christ impinge on our lives?

2.1 The risen Christ is our indestructible hope because he is the foundation of our faith in all its aspects (1 Cor 15:12-18). From now on we share a resurrection that operates in our earthly life and eternal life (1 Cor 15:19-28). The Gospel moves towards the resurrection as its conclusion, required by the divinity of Christ revealed. We must reread the story of the mortal Jesus in the light of the glory of his immortality. We must confirm our faith in the risen Christ as the most decisive acquisition in our whole Christian experience. It is of course above the mystery of the cross, which gains its meaning from it. Only then will we be able to give the reason for our hope. We must look out for the doubts caused by the momentary dismay the cross might cause us (in any of its forms), doubts which obstruct the power to rise from the tomb. Let us not forget the Lord's conversation on the road to Emmaus (Lk 24:13-55) and the recurring dialectic of the paschal rhythm (Phil 2:5-11). Let us be bearers to the world and human beings in despair for so many reasons, of the indestructible hope of the risen Christ, instead of being 'prophets of doom'.

2.2. *The risen Christ is our model of holiness* because he brings us a new life in all our mediocrity and limitation. In this life we are dead to sin and all its manifestations and open to new ways of existing, which we must continually develop (Rom 6:3-11; Col 2:6-11 and 3:1-17). In becoming like the Son we will do the Father's will and also become integrated as persons through our share in Jesus' personality, the Son of man. The whole principle and foundation [23] is illuminated by this risen life. Being saints means living in a state of resurrection, which in practice simply means applying the 'happiness criteria' to our everyday life. Holiness and justice are indissolubly linked. Only the holiness of Jesus confronting the injustice of selfish sin to the death, allows us to enjoy the resurrection, which now appears as a state of justice in all spheres. To phrase it simply, the risen Christ puts all things in their place and reminds us that all holiness that does not engage in the struggle for justice is vain.

2.3. *The risen Christ is our apostolic good news,* as he appears in all the great speeches in the Acts of the Apostles, especially the first one by Peter in 2:14-36 with its rousing insistence on his victory over death. We must go through life announcing the power of resurrection hidden in all human beings, sharing in the incarnate person of the Word. We can all rise again to goodness, justice, mercy, truth etc., because these resurrections have occurred in Jesus and we can prolong them in history. *Loving means living beyond death*, because it means putting the love of a risen God at the heart of life and things. In our daily *lives we must live as if risen from the dead.*

2.4. *The risen Christ is our peace received and given,* as in the Lord's farewell at the Last Supper (Jn 14:19-23). And there are many other passages in which peace is a formal greeting. This means that in spite of all our weaknesses and mistakes, peace should be our permanent state as believers.

Believers should also give peace to their brothers and sisters, as a sign of faith. But, beware! 'Risen peace' is the fruit of a life surrendered to love, which we reflected on in the previous propositions. *The way of the cross is the way of peace.* (That is why Jesus said our peace is different from the world's, which is so often founded on selfish balancing.) Peace is won through an all-out struggle against all forms of selfishness, which is our daily cross.

So the resurrection shapes us if we accept it as adults. Living in a state of resurrection shapes us as different people amidst the sin of the world, continually struggling for love to the end. But all this depends on a radical conviction: that the daily struggle for love is the fertile source of joy in our lives, a joy which shares in the unending joy of the glorious Christ.

3. *The resurrection finishes in the Exercises with the 'contemplation to attain love'* [230-237]

The exerciser reaches fulfilment in a way of life that Ignatius describes as a loving relationship between lover and beloved, giving priority to practical over verbal love [230-231]. This 'loving relationship' is the ripe fruit of the 'resurrection state' we have already discussed. In this state those who have risen with Christ contemplate the whole of creation and their whole life as a 'gift of the Father' and in consequence surrender themselves completely to the Father [233-237]. This is the context for the well known prayer 'Take, Lord', as a summing up of all the Exercises in an absolute surrender to the Father's will, a total victory over selfishness. Praying this prayer and truly adopting it means adopting the whole and thereby setting ourselves in the 'third way of humility' [167], the height of Christian love. It is appropriate here to go through all these Ignatian paragraphs slowly, to establish a definitive relationship with God based on love that is stronger than all our selfishness.

There is something else. The Father's plan is that this saving love relationship should be revealed to the whole world, because it has been fulfilled in the fullness of Christ the saviour (Rom 8:19-25). For the world and its people a moment of new birth has arrived, which can develop its hidden potentialities. This means we are instruments of revelation and hope. We must communicate the content of the 'contemplation to attain love' to all, as the essence of our relationship with God.

Thus the exerciser who has assimilated Christ's fullness knows full well what he or she is and what stand needs to be taken. These questions also arose in the principle and foundation. The Exercises bring us back to the reality stated at their beginning but now in terms of a deep identification with Jesus, the risen Christ, fullness, which is the believer's final state. *This is God's will*, which we are pursuing during this experience and our whole life. That is why we said the Exercises were not just one more act of Christian devotion but meant taking the risk of being profoundly transformed and restructured, through a radical reconsideration of our daily and fundamental values. The paschal mystery has brought us here: to living with creatures in the style of the Lord Jesus, manifestation of the Father's will. And properly speaking, this is not indifference but an absolute differentiation in accordance with Jesus Christ.

Suggestions for particular reflection

— Do I experience Jesus' resurrection as the final flowering of the Father's will, which is the foundation of Christocentric unity and cosmic fellowship? Or do I see life negatively?

— Do I experience in prayer, in the community and in social life an actual encounter with Jesus Christ as comforter? Or do I merely store up negative experiences which make me sad and look at life pessimistically?

— Is it Mary who reveals to me from her own experience the mystery of the risen Christ? Or do I fail to see a 'Christly' virgin in my devotion to Mary?

— Am I capable of reviewing my humiliations and painful defeats in the light of the resurrection? Or am I overwhelmed by them so that the 'paschal rhythm' of my life is destroyed?

— Do I regard myself and others with indestructible hope, based on sharing in Christ's resurrection? Or do I prefer to wallow in my limitations, proclaiming a negative and masochistic Gospel?

— Do I see the universe as a place of resurrection so that I feel its positive and optimistic appeal? Or do I look at temporal realities pessimistically, as irreparably damaged by sin?

— Do I say the prayer 'Take, Lord' [234] as a generous response to so much fatherly love? Or am I still wary of surrendering to God's love in a way appropriate to one who knows all good comes from him?

Because the risen Christ has died he is something radically new and disconcerting for a secular society like ours. Therefore to bear witness through a life converted to hope and joy to the innovating fact of the resurrection is the greatest contribution I can make to changing the world. The routine of despair and the victims of gross selfishness may acquire the hope of transforming unjust structures, a hope whose characteristics are also revolutionary. We must constantly repeat that everything has changed radically, because Christian transformation begins with the resurrection but by our fear and distrust we believers can prevent its completion. This is our gravest historical responsibility.

≈ ≈ ≈

The ascension: The paschal mystery as glory. Heaven

1. Jesus said to his disciples at the Last Supper: 'Now I am leaving the world and returning to the Father' (Jn 16:28). The Son's true home is his Father's house, in union with the Spirit, as a mystery of trinitarian love. This means that while the whole Gospel is an affirmation of God's immanence in Jesus Christ, the Gospel ends by confirming what we already knew since the incarnation, that in Jesus there also lies the mystery of divine transcendence and ultimately this mystery is what defines him. Therefore our contemplation of the 'history of Jesus Christ' requires that we conclude it with his ascension into glory. The resurrection attains its fulfilment in the ascension, as Paul shows in his paschal hymn in Philippians (2:9-11), a hymn summing up the Lord's 'incarnation trajectory'.

2. *New Testament data characterising the ascension.* If we look at the various ascension narratives in the New Testament (Mt 28:16-20; Lk 24:36-49; Mk 16:14-20; Jn 20:19-23; Acts 1:9-11) we realise the following points, all of which are very important to our faith and the Church's life:

– Jesus Christ only attains definitive Lordship when he is glorified at the right hand of the Father, recovering his primary state.

– The behaviour he requires from his disciples is not ecstatic contemplation but active preaching of the Gospel.

– The ascension corresponds with the gift of the Spirit, as Jesus promised a number of times at the Last Supper. The Spirit will help the disciples in their task of proclaiming the Good News.

– In the omnipotent power of his lordship Jesus Christ himself remains with his own people, co-operating with them in the task of salvation.

Thus the ascension has a double message of joy and

commitment: joy at the Lord's final triumph and commitment because our response to his lordship must be to co-
operate in proclaiming his kingdom. We must not surrender
to empty spiritualism. Jesus Christ and his Spirit will help us
in our task 'until the end of time'. So we could say that these
ascension narratives concentrate all Christian spirituality in
human history, as a person in tension between the 'beyond'
of the glorified Christ and the 'here and now' of preaching
the Gospel. We must be faithful in two ways: to the glory we
expect in the final kingdom and to the proclamation of this
kingdom in human space and time.

The Church, the historical body of its glorified Lord,
must live in this state of committed joy. It is significant that
only when Jesus returns to the Father does he send his Spirit
at Pentecost to hold together the primitive community in
Jerusalem (Acts 2:1-4). Through Peter this community rapidly begins simply to tell the story of Jesus Christ. Our
Church is the ripe fruit of the ascension, as a Trinitarian
mystery passed on to the disciples of the Paschal Lamb. It
too must maintain a difficult tension between its heavenly
and its earthly character. It is the pilgrim people of God, in
the image of the long pilgrimage of Jesus its head, as described by John in the prologue to his Gospel.

3. *From the ascension arises the mystery of our own
glorification which we call heaven.* The believer who has
shared in the Lord's death and resurrection will also share in
his heavenly glorification. This will fulfil everything said by
Jesus about eternal life (recall the intimate relationship with
the body and blood of the Eucharist). But let us look at this
question in two ways:

3.1. *The basis of the believer's heavenly glorification
appears in various texts.* We summarise a few: Col 1:27:
Jesus Christ hope of glory; Rom 8:18-33: Jesus Christ communicates glory to us; Rom 2:22-33: God gives eternal life

by means of Jesus Christ his Son. Only to the extent that we live identified with the Lord's paschal mystery can we enjoy the eternal fulfilment of his glory. This is our final identification with him in his Father's house.

3.2. *So what will heaven be like?* According to 1 Thessalonians 4:13-18 glory or 'heaven' will mean 'being always with the Lord'. This final absolute certainty should bring us comfort in the difficulties of our lives. Heaven is the fulfilment of our encounter with the Lord, which we looked at when we spoke about calling. It consists in being 'with me'. But let us note something else. The Pauline text always speaks of 'us'. That is, it gives the happiness of heaven a communal and ecclesial character. There will be fellowship there too. For if we enjoy and possess the fullness of love we cannot fail also to enjoy a full exchange of friendship.

Even in our pilgrim life in the Church on earth we experience something of the glorious heavenly reality of each and every human being who loves the Lord. We do not live as people without hope. The truth is we are journeying there, a place where we shall be all together without any tears, enjoying (through vision and no longer in faith) the presence of the Father, the Son and the Spirit. So we conclude this contemplation by giving thanks for having been incorporated even now in the mystery of the Trinity, which will become visible in the life we hope for and believe in as eternal.

Suggestions for particular reflection

— What definitive image of Jesus do I have when I confront life's difficulties? Do I resort to the revealed fact that Jesus is the one who triumphs over all selfishness in the glory of the Father?

— Do I accept the inevitable tension between immanence and transcendence and heaven and earth as implicit in

our situation between here and there? Or do I prefer to stick
with just one of the elements, thereby upsetting God's plan
for me?

— In moments of depression do I recall the hope of
heavenly glory, not so much as a reward but as the joy of
being with the Lord of my life? Or when I am depressed do I
ignore this horizon of hope?

— Do I have an image of the Church linked to eternal
life, in the sense that our sinful Church will finally be holy
when it enters fully into the glory of its head? Or have I
impoverished the holiness of the Church with useless and
frivolous criticisms?

— Do I think from time to time about heaven? Or am I
basically a believer for whom eternal life does not mean
anything consistent?

Eighth day:
Plan of future life

Morning prayer. 'Prayer for today'.

Work for the morning. 'Personal plan of future life'.

Proposition for the afternoon. 'The Church of faith, the Spirit, Mary and the believing community, our Church. After that, comment on the 'conclusion to the Exercises'.

At the Eucharist after communion. 'Prayer for the end of the Exercises' and the 'Prayer of Ignatius'.

Prayer for today

There was a day,
which I now contemplate with acute nostalgia,
when you returned to the glory of the Father.

The curious thing is, Lord,
that your going was both
sadness of being orphaned and enthusiasm for the future.
Because you did not just go away
leaving an infinite emptiness behind you.
First you made us become the Church.
Then you gave us the Spirit.
The two consummations
of your evangelical and Trinitarian life.

Today in my day
I still long for your presence.
I discover you in the fellowship of the Church
and I love you with the strongest spiritual power.

I am certain, Lord:
my faith in you is through love for my brothers and sisters,
leading me to historical fulfilment
in your body,
which is the believing community of the Church.

Your painful departure
gave us the gift of active faith,
which serves the only Lord
by serving this Lord's friends.

Today in my day you are in others.
Today in my day you are in the Church.
Today in my day you are the Holy Spirit.

Your absence is a mysterious presence
because you surround me,
and I see you with new eyes.

Give me just one grace:
that I may never lose that yearning memory,
but that I may also never lose my love today.
Because you are not here... but you are.
You are the Church, spread all over the earth.
And you are Spirit, poured out into all hearts.

≈ ≈ ≈

Personal plan of future life

I think that at this point in the Exercises we must confront
ourselves in order to draw some conclusions about the future. For this we can make use of the experience we have
had during these days. I am proposing to dedicate the whole
morning of this last day to sketching the characteristics of
what we could call a 'personal plan of future life'. We must
fall neither into rationalism nor Pelagian voluntarism. We
must simply reflect quietly on our future and its Christian
dynamic.

This involves two different tasks. The first and principal
one is to draw up the main lines to organise the structure of
my Christian life. We should spend as much time as necessary, because the other task can be done on another day after
the Exercises. The second much more pragmatic task is the
drawing up of a sort of 'decalogue', summing up the most
common situations and questions occurring in my daily life.
For this we must examine ourselves in detail. Both these

tasks are important and should help us to prevent our experience of the Exercises draining away to nothing in a few days, as so often happens.

In the interests of organisation it can be helpful to spend a long time reflecting in the same room, taking a few notes if this helps us fix our ideas. Later it will be convenient to present all these conclusions to the Lord in an atmosphere of prayer, praying that our future may be accepted or corrected. In any case, it is clear that the work proposed for this last morning should be done only insofar as it helps the particular exerciser. Therefore, if this work complicates your life in a negative way, you should not do it and spend the time in presenting to Jesus the whole task of the Exercises and your desire to know, love and follow him.

1. *Drawing up the main lines*

Now that we have nearly come to the end of our Exercises, we must try to replace the image we had at the beginning, which should have been rectified by various elements in our spiritual experience. In the light of this experience we should ask ourselves what broad lines do I see for my future life as demanded by the Lord in this particular moment of my pilgrimage? In other words, what is God's will for me now? What we usually call proposals are usually left to later daily decisions. Now we must try to see where the Lord is leading us, which will emerge later in these more detailed decisions.

This is the moment to look through notes taken on previous days, summarising the best illuminations granted by the Spirit. We should also go over all the material of the Exercises to see if any new spiritual insight occurs. We should do this work quietly without haste, remembering that these 'main lines for our future life' should never be too many. There should be two, three or four at most, because these are substantial elements upon which to rest all my daily experience of spiritual life at this moment in my life. If anyone asks what I mean by these 'lines', I reply by giving a few examples. There is the need to bear very much in mind my relationship with God my creator and Father; keep alive the structure of grace and temptation; from the viewpoint of the incarnation contemplate reality as something positive; the centrality of the person of Jesus Christ in my life; the beatitudes as 'reference points' of Christian life; accepting the dynamic of the 'paschal rhythm'; the importance of Mary's intercession; and so on. I repeat that these 'lines' are very personal.

The results of this work will create the features of my new Christian image, its main lines. I endeavour to restructure myself both inwardly and outwardly on the basis of my experience of faith. Beware: we must continually submit these features or lines for revision, according to the development of my spiritual life, in a very serious and honest atmosphere of spiritual discernment. Thus the Exercises become a school for believing life, capable of forming the inner person as a radical whole. And of course this inward formation will then relate to outward behaviour.

2. *A decalogue of the most essential aspects of life to test where my present 'restructuring' is actually leading*

2.1. Is my community a place of Christian and institutional experience and of human satisfaction and rest? Or has it become (have I turned it into) a sort of hotel? What are my community attitudes and responsibility in these questions? What particular reasons do I find for behaving as I do?

2.2. Do I always keep alive the original experience of my calling (maturing it in accordance with the course of my life)? Or do I consider it is something that just happened and does not concern me now? Do I frequently reconfront the obligations of my calling?

2.3. Is my prayer a personal and communal encounter with the mystery of God in Jesus Christ through the Spirit? Or has it become purely formal? Or have I even abandoned it or cut it right down? Why have I abandoned it or cut it down? Do I offer the – invalid – excuse of lack of time?

2.4. Do I feel an urgent pressure to proclaim the Gospel (under whatever form)? Or have I become completely professionalised or spiritualised? Do I engage in any priestly or evangelising activity specifically as such? What?

2.5. Do I take responsibility without excuses for my profession? Or do I fail to put as much into it as I should? Do I continue to take responsibility for it through 'permanent education' of an organised kind? Is it also hindered by excess of work to which I devote myself entirely all day long?

2.6. Do I sympathise, suffer with the problems of society and individuals at all levels? Or do I remain on the sidelines of what happens to the people of my time... as if it did not concern me? Have I accepted the dangerous loss of this 'evangelical horizon'?

2.7. Am I aware of new cultural alternatives (intellectual, artistic, or new forms of life and customs)? Or do I barely concede them any importance, perhaps because I do not even want to know? Do I read any of the key books of the year? Do I assimilate the new mentality? Do I compare it with my previous positions? Do I allow myself the necessary margin for 'on-going formation' in this respect?

2.8. Do I manage to educate myself in theology and spirituality or does the gap between my sacred and secular knowledge widen all the time? There is no room for excuses here. So why have I perhaps abandoned all this? Do I realise that this abandonment affects my spiritual life, the coherence of my Christianity and my potential as an apostle?

2.9. Do I make my vows a means of being available for Christly and apostolic love or are they just a useless burden? Have I organised my life according to my tastes and to do what I like? What place does 'spiritual accompaniment' have in my life?

2.10. Is the Eucharist the crucial moment of my daily activity? Does it sum up my whole life? Or have I let it become a monotonous repetition of certain almost useless gestures? Do I take part in it every day or only when... work permits?

Note. Each person should add other questions which may be absolutely essential to form the basis of daily life, so that the dynamism of the Exercises may continue.

≈ ≈ ≈

The Church of faith, the Spirit, Mary and the community of the Church

1. *Introduction: a charisma to develop*

1.1. *The encounter with Jesus in human time and space* takes place fully in the Church, the historical body of the Lord (1 Cor 12:27), above all through the Holy Spirit, who gives vitality and coherence to the body of the Church, as we shall see. So the Church is the environment in which the total experience of the paschal mystery occurs, in which we live and die in accordance with the cross and resurrection of Jesus Christ, for others, fighting for faith and the justice demanded by this faith. In consequence, the Church is not one 'possibility' among others for the believer. It is a genuine necessity, because in it we receive the fundamental grace of baptism, of which the Church is the bearer. This grace 'christens' us for ever. This means that all the baptised are the Church, and even though constructive and loving criticism is appropriate so that it does not fall away and become unfaithful to its essence, we must begin with our own conversion if we intend to convert the Church. We should have no truck with parallel Churches, but work hard daily from within the one Church, which we call 'Catholic'.

1.2. *Between charisma and evolution.* The Church's life like that of the whole body takes place in a necessary and enriching tension which affects all without exception:

a. On the one hand deep faithfulness to its evangelical charisma, just as those who had handled the Word of life were faithful (1 Jn 1:1-14); a charisma that extends to tradition and the magisterium.

b. On the other hand a courageous and decisive risk to deepen and interpret the charisma in virtue of the signs of the times, given that the Spirit unfolds the infinite riches of the Lord throughout the length and breadth of human history (cf the Council of Jerusalem in Acts 15:1-35).

In faithfulness to the charisma we must also allow it to evolve, avoiding the mistakes of becoming stuck or too hasty advance, which in opposite ways destroy the Church's historical rhythm, even though they try to justify themselves with apparently respectable motives. Here too we need 'spiritual discernment'. In other words, we must go deeper and deeper into the charismatic precisely in order to be faithful to it. We must reject both 'integrism' and 'progressism' as short cut attempts to 'be the Church'. We must remain very open to the Church's prophets, who perhaps in rather imperfect form detect the new ways of the Lord. One unmistakable sign of such brave prophecy will be the obvious shadow of the cross on it, making it biblical.

Everything we have said about the Church's charisma and evolution must be applied to the different religious families, who need to adapt their founding faith to the requirements of the course of history. Given the complexity of the times in which we live, we need large doses of spiritual discernment but also to realise that if we are unwilling to take risks we are bound to stagnate. The yearning for security is the great enemy of all religious experience because the Gospel is a permanent risk trusting in God.

Note finally what we have already suggested in mentioning the prophetic: that sharing in this urgent task of taking the Church forward as well as its consecrated families, will entail persecution and the cross. We must be aware of this in advance. We must set our eyes on the final fullness of Jesus Christ and not on the littleness of our present human limitations, which share in the sin of the world. This is how we must love the Church. This is how we must love our religious families. Anything else is evasion to the right or left, which lead to nothing but damaging disasters.

2. *Birth of the Church: its essential sources*

These essential sources are simultaneous and united in complementary fashion in time and space. All together they form a 'spectrum' which constitute the activity of the body of the Church.

2.1. *Faith* (Mt 16:13-20) and love (Jn 21:15-17) in and for Jesus Christ. This takes us back to paragraph [104] in the Exercises.

2.2. *The active presence of the Holy Spirit:*
a. who shapes the Church at Pentecost (Acts 2:1-4) as a community of believers in Jesus Christ and preachers of his Gospel.

b. who develops a series of teaching tasks in the body of the Church, as revealed by Jesus Christ at the Last Supper:

– Jn 14:15-17: the Holy Spirit as companion and counsellor (no individualism here) and possessor of truth (be wary of dangerous subjectivism) and rejection of the world (help in discernment).

– Jn 14:25-26: the Holy Spirit as counsellor and companion, but also as teacher of all things (beware of 'partial Christians') and reminder of Jesus ('*memoria fidei*'). With this Holy Spirit we can understand the Exercises as always integrated into the whole Christian experience and intimately related with the person of the Lord.

– Jn 15:26-27: The Holy Spirit, the counsellor and companion and possessor of truth, is the one who helps us bear witness to the cause of Jesus. He stands at the very centre of our work of preaching to the Gospel.

– Jn 16:12-15: The Holy Spirit, the spirit of truth, will lead us into all truth (again beware of partialism), he will interpret the future for us (the signs of the times and new prophets), and above all he will interpret Jesus for us (against false interpreters). He will enable us to contemplate the risen Christ in the crucified.

Thus the person of the Holy Spirit is at the centre of the Church's dynamism, intimately related with the most delicate aspects of the historical body of Jesus Christ: truth, the future, the Gospel. It would therefore be a serious mistake to forget this most important protagonist of the Church's vital structure. Nevertheless when great problems beset us in the Church do we keep in mind the Holy Spirit in our prayers and discernment?

c. Who constantly appears in Paul's writings:

– Rom 8:15-17: tells us about fatherhood and adoption, enabling us to pray deeply with these in mind. (He is the master of prayer.)

– Rom 8:1-14: He is the possessor of the 'Christly life' in all its dimensions, enabling us to overcome evil.

– Rom 8:26-7: Again he is the master of prayer, because he is the one who knows what we should ask intimately of God.
– 1 Cor 12:1-3: He enables us to confess Jesus Christ, as if he were at the depths of our life of faith.
– 1 Cor 12:4-11: He is the giver of the different ecclesial charismata, which make the Church 'balanced'.
– 1 Cor 12:12-14: He creates Church unity, but from the previous diversity of gifts.
– 1 Cor 2:9-16: He is the one who reveals God's depths to us, in a clear and certain discernment.

We must stress once more that the protagonism of the Holy Spirit in the Church is extraordinarily striking. To the point where our behaviour as members of the Church should be as mere listeners to the Holy Spirit, because everything we need we receive from him. Nevertheless the Holy Spirit is widely ignored by Catholics.

2.3. *Mary's model motherhood*

– As a discerner of God's will in freedom when she showed her faith in the annunciation at Nazareth (Lk 1:26-38).
– As one who knows her son intimately in daily contemplation of his life as she helped him grow up (Lk 2:1-19).
– As a preacher of Jesus in Bethlehem by giving birth to him (Lk 2:1-20) and in Cana by being aware (Jn 2:1-12).
– As a co-redeemer in the paschal mystery. She risked loving to the end (Jn 19:25-27).

Mary is the womb from which our Church is born, both physically and morally because of her special relationship with her Son, the head of the Church. Therefore our Church has recognised her as its Mother, not merely spiritually but theologically, with a biblical foundation.

2.4. *The early believing community.* From the beginning there was a group of followers of Jesus living in common and remembering the crucified and risen Jesus. These were a sort of pre-Church. Pentecost meant their transformation into a community as such, as we shall see. But it is important to stress that even before this there was a group of believers. The experience of Jesus Christ was never individual but communal (Acts 1:12-14 and 2:1-4).

3. *Characteristics of the ecclesial community its vital structure*

The Acts of the Apostles show us the whole diverse wealth of the primitive Christian community, which was articulated in accordance with certain features that continue to operate in our day and can never be given up. (Here too we have the theme of complementarity because none of the characteristics is less valuable than another):

3.1. *The Church as a living community (social structure).* In Acts 2:42-47; 4:32-35 and 5:12-16 we see a human group united by certain particular features which caused the group to increase (2:47). Are these the criteria of our present day communities with all due historical adaptations? What are our distinctive social features in a secular society?

3.2. *The Church as a community of charismata (functional structure).* From the beginning we find the already mentioned tension between the different charismata, which produce a definite confrontation between the brothers and sisters. But charity is retained as the fundamental charisma (Acts 15:1-35; 1 Cor 12). Do we accept charismatic tension as a communal search for the ways of the Lord? Do we give due importance to spiritual discernment? This is the context for the theme of obedience in consecrated life, which we consider later.

3.3. *The Church, a community for preaching the Gospel (historical structure).* Acts are a witness to the fact that the Church was born to proclaim the Gospel in history. This task justifies the existence of the community, and brings about the full encounter between human beings and the man Jesus (2:14-41; 3:11-26; 7:1-58; 10:34-43; 13:16-41; 17:22-31). Are our communities really open to a daily and committed proclaiming of the Gospel? Or are they closed in upon themselves and lacking in apostolic dynamism? All community is for mission. But we must also remember that all mission peters out without a community to welcome and empower it.

We must live in the community of the Church in order to reproduce in our situation today the early Christian reality, which was directly touched by the pure grace of charisma. We must reproduce in our time Jesus' Gospel summons, which called the twelve to be with him and to go out to work for him (Mk 3:13-19).

4. *Consecrated obedience*

Obedience has always been a problem in the Church, perhaps because it is so closely bound up with freedom. On this question we may say:

4.1. Obedience in the Church should be seen as a very special link with the community of the Church through representatives elected by her by listening to what the people of God feel. Therefore without a sane theology of the Church as people articulated in a permanent dialectic between top and bottom, obedience will be subject to an unacceptable monarchism.

4.2. Consecrated obedience is justified as a deepening of the Church's general charisma in a particular form, by means of a person who can both understand this charisma and instigate it among others. Authorities which are merely imposed, that is, without authentic discernment, are not of much use for anything, except to make things more complicated and worry people.

To sum up, the Church's authority is a community service to encourage in freedom all kinds of characteristics in the Church. It therefore should be respected but may also be criticised in fellowship, because in the end authority can never be imposed in a totalitarian manner on sincere fellowship. The same goes for consecrated families, the religious orders. The fact that this is difficult is another matter. But either we must learn to rule in accordance with these criteria or we will be involved in repeated problems which have no solution. This would obviously be a danger to people's vocations.

Appendix: Rules for thinking with the Church [352-370]

Very practically Ignatius concludes the Exercises with some rules. 'In order to think with the Church militant we should keep the following rules.' He gives eighteen rules.

This is because Ignatius realises from his own experiences that in the Christian's daily life the most difficult thing will be to relate to the living and diverse body of the Church. (We may recall his own time, full of strong light and shade.) He then draws up some rules to facilitate in day to day activity a good understanding between the believer and his or her Church. It is a good idea to read them. But of course in their historical context. Obviously, they need to be updated but we should keep their toughness, which can only be understood as showing a great love for the Lord's body in history.

Suggestions for particular reflection

– Am I convinced that my encounter with the historical Jesus is through the body of the Church, which is also historical? Or have I split these two realities?

– Do I take the discerning risk both in the Church and in my institution of conjugating faithfulness and renewal? Do I manage neither to 'stick in the mud' nor to be too hasty? Do I also allow for discerning prophecy from the cross?

– Do I really live with the springs of the eternal Church: Jesus Christ, the Spirit, Mary, the community? Or have I invented other sources for the Church, which lack any guarantee and which I may also try to impose upon others?

– Do I also live in accordance with the characteristics of the primitive Church and try to transpose them into my time? Do I also keep the dimension of community as essential for the historical Church?

– Do I obey with respect and sound critical sense? Or am I permanently in disagreement?

– Do I give more real importance to my partial institution than to the Church as a whole?

– Do I construct the Church in accordance with my particular conversion instead of always criticising it like an outsider?

≈ ≈ ≈

Conclusion to the Exercises

Here we conclude our Christian experience in the style of Ignatius of Loyola (who is simply one among many others). From the beginning we have confronted ourselves, as individual and collective persons needing to resolve our fundamental problem. What is the ultimate meaning of our life, a life which in our case is also a life of believing? Our work has been analysis, search and resolutions to discover God's will for us at this moment of our life. This is the primary Christian question.

Looking back over the way we have come we find a few things stand out as absolutely necessary and indispensable. First, the encounter with Jesus Christ in our own particular history. This is the great radical adventure, which can change our lives from lukewarm to fervent. Secondly, there is the Christian community as the environment in which to have this encounter in a charismatic space-time tension. Then there is the Holy Spirit, whom we discovered to be at work in Mary as the instrument of all this, the soul of the Church. Jesus Christ, community and Spirit offer spiritual discernment in historical conflicts. They are indispensable in order to help us discover moment by moment the course we should take as believers in doing the work of the Gospel today. Let us not be hasty in resolving spiritual questions. We should be prudent in the only certainty we have: viz, that of the good Spirit who is present to us in mysterious but perceptible ways.

We must live in a continual state of restructuring. Always passing from death to life in accordance with the paschal rhythm, which is central to the Christly experience. We must be converted from selfishness to love: this is the essential task running through our relationship with the three above-mentioned realities. This conversion, which must show in all our life, is the only proof that the Gospel has worked on us. Where God is present there love is, love which is also justice. Our restructuring must therefore include others, for whom we must struggle. To the death, death on the cross. Like the Lord Jesus.

In order for all this to take place we must break nets and chains, we must leave our boats and our fishing, and wait in hope. And without any doubt Jesus Christ will come.

≈ ≈ ≈

Prayer at the end of the Exercises

Eternal Lord of all things,
once again I come to the end of these days of prayer
in which I have followed Ignatius Loyola.
I want to say goodbye to you
with enormous gratitude.
Jesus Christ of history, my whole life
is struck by the sword of your Gospel
which invites me to meet you,
to know you better, love you better, follow you better.
So I can live as you lived:
in your style of the Sermon on the Mount
and the Last Supper.

I am very aware of the self-abandonment
involved in such a decision
because it means total submission
to the Father's will,
which will be revealed in the particular details
of my whole life,
if I have a minimum of spiritual awareness.
But in any case, here I am,
ready for anything,   ,
ready to follow you,
my supreme and eternal captain, Jesus.

Make me disencumber myself of everything
in order to be able to proclaim you in freedom
(this will be my poverty).
Make me not marry anyone or anything
in order to consecrate myself to you alone
(this will be my virginity).
Make me capable of humiliating my will
to serve you in the community of faith and works
(this will be my obedience).

Show me the inner and the practical power
of my three vows
as something liberating, fulfilling and joyful.

I want to do all this in the Church,
the historical body of your own person,
and also in humanity,
the environment of your permanent incarnation.
So give me a sense of the historical moment
to discover and admit the signs of the times.
Henceforth let me change my points of view,
in order to do my work in the society of today.

Knowing that I am in the world without being of the world
but taking the risk of committing myself
to the reality, as you did in your life.
Thus I will be able to live intensely
the paschal mystery.
And in the pain of service and revolution
I shall find the joy and reward of glory.
Contemplating how all things come from above
and surrendering myself to you
with the hope that you will take all of me.

Today, at the end of the Exercises,
I place in the hands of our mother, Mary of Nazareth,
the deep conversion of my whole life,
my conscious wish to be an honest believer,
my consecrated commitment.
And I ask as my only possession,
which can fill my whole life,
only to be with you,
Lord of history and my life.

Prayer of Ignatius

Take, Lord, and receive
all my liberty, my memory,
my understanding, all my will,
all I have and possess.
You gave it to me,
I give it back to you, Lord.
Everything is yours,
use it as you will.
Give me your love and grace,
which is sufficient for me. [234]

The Spiritual Exercises of
St Ignatius of Loyola

Complete Text

Anima Christi

Soul of Christ, sanctify me.
Body of Christ, save me.
Blood of Christ, inebriate me,
Water from the side of Christ, wash me.
Passion of Christ, strengthen me.
O good Jesus, hear me.
Permit me not to be separated from thee.
From the wicked foe defend me.
At the hour of my death call me
And bid me come to thee
That with thy saints I may praise thee
For ever and ever. Amen.

INTRODUCTORY OBSERVATIONS

These observations are intended to provide some understanding of the spiritual exercises which follow and to guide both the retreat director and the retreatant.

[1] The term 'Spiritual Exercises' is used for any method of examination of conscience, meditation, contemplation, vocal and mental prayer, and other spiritual activities which will be mentioned later. Just as riding, walking and running are exercises for the body, so too preparing and disposing the soul to rid itself of all inordinate attachments, and then seeking and finding God's will in your life for the salvation of our soul, are called spiritual exercises.

[2] The one who explains to another the method and order for meditating or contemplating must treat accurately the subject of the contemplation or meditation, adhering to the main points and adding only a brief summary. Then one is able to contemplate and grasp the essence of the subject with far greater clarity. This may happen either through one's own reasoning or through illumination by divine grace. This is bound to produce greater spiritual relish and benefit than if the director had given a lengthy exposition of the subject. For it is not much knowledge that fills and satisfies the soul, but the intimate feeling and relishing of truth.

[3] In all the following spiritual exercises we use the intellect or understanding and the will for expressing love. However, when we use our will in mental or vocal colloquy with God our Lord or his saints, greater reverence is required than when we use the intellect for understanding.

[4] Four weeks are allotted for the exercises that follow, which correspond to the four parts into which they are divided. The first part is for the consideration and contemplation of sins; the second considers the life of Christ our Lord up to and including Palm Sunday; the

third the passion of Christ our Lord; the fourth his resurrection and
ascension, to which are appended three methods of prayer. However,
each week need not necessarily consist of seven or eight days. For it
happens that sometimes in the first week some are slower in finding
what they seek, namely, contrition, sorrow and tears for their sins.
Some may be more diligent than others, and some are disturbed and
tested by various spirits. So it may be necessary sometimes to shorten
the week and at other times to lengthen it. The same applies to all the
weeks that follow as we seek to achieve the aim of these exercises.
However, it should be done in approximately thirty days.

[5]   Those who do the exercises will benefit greatly by going into
them with great courage and generosity towards their Creator and
Lord, offering him their total will and freedom, so that God may
dispose of them and their possessions according to his most holy will.

[6]   When the director of the exercises sees that the person doing
them experiences no spiritual consolations or desolations, and is not
troubled by any spirits, the director should carefully question the
person doing the exercises as to whether he is doing them at the right
time and in the right manner. Likewise he should inquire whether he
is diligent in the observance of the additional directions. He will
demand a detailed account of each one of these points. Paragraphs
316-324 speak of consolation and desolation. The additional directions are given in paragraphs 73-90.

[7]   If the director of the exercises sees that the retreatant is desolate
or tempted, he must not be hard or harsh with him. He should be
gentle and kind, giving encouragement to go on. He should show him
the wiles of the enemy of human nature, and make him prepare for
the consolation to come.

[8]   If the director perceives that the one who is making the exercises
has need of experiencing desolation, the wiles of the enemy and
consolations, he should explain to him the rules given in the first and
second weeks, which are for the discernment of spirits [313-327 and
328-336].

[9]   During the first week, if the retreatant is a person inexperienced
in spiritual things, and if he is patently and grossly tempted for
example by vision of the obstacles to his progress in the service of
God our Lord, such as troubles, shame and fear of losing worldly

honour etc., the person giving the exercises should not explain to him the rules about various spirits in the second week. For, although the rules for the first week will benefit him, those for the Second Week will do him harm, because what they deal with is too subtle and advanced for him to grasp.

[10] When the director of the exercises perceives that the retreatant is being assailed and tempted under the appearance of good, then it is appropriate to explain to him the rules of the second week, which we mentioned above. For generally the enemy of human nature tempts us more under the appearance of good when we are exercising ourselves in the illuminative way. This refers to the second week. Instead, when he is exercising himself in the purgative way as directed in the first week, the enemy does not tempt him as much under the appearance of good.

[11] When the retreatant is doing the exercises in the first week, it is better for him not to know anything about what is to be done in the Second Week. Thus he should strive to attain what he seeks in the First Week as if he hoped to find no good in the Second.

[12] The director of the exercises must insist with the retreatant that, since he is to spend an hour for each of the five daily exercises or contemplations, he must take care that he can be truthfully satisfied that he has persevered in the exercise for a full hour. Rather than not use the full time, let him exceed one hour. For the enemy tries his best to cause this hour of contemplation, meditation or prayer to be shortened.

[13] The retreatant should also be warned that while it is easy and pleasant to remain in contemplation for a full hour in the time of consolation, it is very difficult to do so in the time of desolation. Therefore in order to withstand desolation and conquer temptations, the retreatant should always remain in the exercise a little longer than a full hour. He will thus gain the habit not only of resisting the enemy but defeating him.

[14] If the director of the exercises sees that the retreatant is receiving consolation and progressing enthusiastically, he should warn him not to be rash and hasty in making any promise or vow. The more unstable in character the retreatant is the more he needs to be warned and admonished. For although it may be right to encourage someone

to embrace the religious life, in which vows of obedience, poverty and chastity are made, and although a good work done under a vow is more meritorious than one done without a vow, nevertheless it is necessary to assess carefully the character and qualities of each individual and the ease or difficulty he would find in carrying out his promises.

[15] The director of the exercises should not urge the retreatant more to poverty or any promises than to the contrary, nor to one state of life more than to another. Outside the exercises, we can rightly encourage everyone who may be suitable to choose chastity, virginity, the religious life and every form of religious perfection. But within the context of the spiritual exercises it is more appropriate and much better that the Creator and Lord should himself communicate to the devout soul in search of the divine will and that he should inflame it with love and dispose it for serving him better. Therefore the director of the exercises should not lean to one side or the other, but maintain a balance to allow the Creator to work directly with the creature and the creature with his Creator and Lord.

[16] If the soul has any inordinate attachment or inclination to any object, it is very beneficial for it to summon all its strength to reach the opposite state to the one which wrongly affects it, so that the Creator and Lord may act with greater certainty in the soul. So if a person is inclined to seek an office or job, not for the honour and glory of God our Lord or for the salvation of souls, but for his own worldly advantage and interest, he must strive for the opposite. Let him by prayer and other spiritual exercises beg God our Lord for the opposite, unless God regulates his desires and changes his former attachment. Hence the reason for desiring or having something must be solely the service, honour and glory of the Divine Majesty.

[17] It is very helpful for the director of the exercises, while not trying to pry into the private thoughts and sins of the retreatant, to be well informed of the various disturbances and thoughts induced by different spirits. Then the director can provide appropriate spiritual exercises to meet the need of a soul thus troubled.

[18] The exercises should be adapted according to the disposition of those wishing to do them, that is, according to their age, education, and intelligence. It is inappropriate to give a simple uneducated person exercises that he cannot comfortably carry out and

benefit from. Likewise each person should be given suitable exercises from which he can derive help and profit.

This someone who wishes no further help than some guidance and the attainment of a certain degree of peace of soul may be given first the particular examination of conscience [24], and then the general examination of conscience [32]. Together with this, he should be given, for half an hour in the morning, the method of prayer on the commandments, the deadly sins etc.[238]. He should be told to confess his sins every week, and receive communion, if possible, every fortnight, or better still, every week if he wishes. This method is more suitable for those who have little natural ability or are illiterate. Each commandment should be explained to them, and also the deadly sins, the commandments of the Church, the use of the five senses and the works of mercy. Likewise if the director of the exercises sees that a person has little aptitude or physical stamina and not much can be expected of him, it is more appropriate to give him some easier exercises as a preparation for confession. He should be given some ways of examining his conscience and a plan for confessing his sins more frequently than in the past. Then he will be able to maintain the spiritual progress he has made. But he should not proceed to such matters as the choice of a way of life or any other exercises not contained in the first week. He will benefit more by confining himself to the exercises mentioned above, as there is no time for him to do everything.

[19] One who is educated or skilled, but engaged in public affairs or business, should daily devote an hour and a half to the exercises. First, the end for which human beings were created should be explained to him, then the particularexamination of conscience may be given half an hour, and after that the general examination of conscience and the method of confessing and receiving holy communion. For an hour each morning for three days he can meditate on the first, second and third sins [45]. After that he can spend the same amount of time on the next three days in the consideration of personal sins [55]. Then for three more days an equal measure of time may be spent in meditating on the punishment due to sin [65]. Along with all these meditations he should be given the ten additional directions [73]. In meditating on the mysteries of Christ our Lord he should observe the same method explained at length later on in the exercises.

[20] Anyone who is less encumbered and wants to make as much progress as possible should be given all the spiritual exercises in the

order in which they are set forth. He will benefit from them according to the degree to which he retreats from friends and acquaintances and earthly cares. He might move out of the house where he lives and stay in another house or room as much privacy as he can. Thus he will be able to go to Mass and vespers, without fear of disruption by his acquaintances. This withdrawal has three main advantages among many others. First, withdrawing from friends and acquaintances and other distractions in order to serve and praise God our Lord, gains a great deal of merit in the eyes of God. Secondly, by withdrawing and not being distracted but concentrating on just one thing, that is, the service his Creator and the good of his own soul, he is able to use his natural faculties more freely and diligently to seek what he so much desires. Thirdly, when the soul is in greater solitude and seclusion, it becomes more fit to approach and be united with its Creator and Lord. And the more closely it is united with the Creator, the more able it is to receive graces and gifts from the infinite goodness of God.

[21] SPIRITUAL EXERCISES

Which have as their purpose the conquest of self and the regulation of one's life in such a way that no decision is made under the influence of any inordinate attachment.

Presupposition

[22] For better cooperation between the director of the spiritual exercises and the retreatant and for better benefit for both, we have to presuppose that every good Christian is more ready to put a good interpretation on another's statement than to condemn it. And if he cannot accept it he should ask what is meant, and if what is meant is wrong, he should correct it with kindness. And if that is not enough, he should seek all appropriate means to make the other person see the truth and thus save the statement from error.

First Week

[23] FIRST PRINCIPLE AND FOUNDATION

Human beings are created to praise, reverence and serve God our Lord and by means of this to save their souls. And the other things in the world are created for us, to help us attain the end for which we were created. Hence it follows that we should use them only to the extent that they help us attain our end, and rid ourselves of them insofar as they hinder us. Therefore it is necessary to make ourselves indifferent to all created things, inasmuch as we are allowed by our free will and not constrained by any prohibition. Thus we should not prefer health to sickness, riches to poverty, honour to dishonour, a long life to a short life, and so on in everything else. We should only desire and choose what is more conducive to the end for which we are created.

[24] DAILY PARTICULAR EXAMINATION OF CONSCIENCE

The particular examination of conscience is to be made daily. It includes three different times of the day and two self-examinations.

First, in the morning. On rising you ought to resolve to guard carefully against the particular sin or defect which you desire to correct in order to improve yourself.

[25] Second, after lunch. You should ask God our Lord to grant what you want, that is, the grace to remember how often you have fallen into that particular sin or defect, and to avoid it in future. Then make the first examination demanding an account from your soul of the particular matter you want to correct and amend. You should review

each hour or period of time beginning from the time you got up to the moment of this examination. Mark the first line of the chart (p 189) with a point for each time you have committed that particular sin or defect. Then resolve to do better up to the time of the second examination.

[26] Third, after supper. Make a second examination in the same way, reviewing as before hour by hour the time between the first examination and the present one. Mark a point on the second line of the same chart for each time you have fallen into that same sin or defect.

[27] FOUR ADDITIONAL DIRECTIONS
These are to serve as a help to the more ready removal of the particular sin or defect.

1. The first direction is that every time you fall into that particular sin or defect, place your hand on your breast, grieving that you have fallen. This can even be done in front of many people, without their being aware of it.

[28] 2. For the second direction, at night look at the first line of the chart which represents the first examination, and the second line of the chart representing the second examination and see if there is an improvement from the first line to the second, that is, from the first examination to the second.

[29] 3. For the third direction, compare the second day with the first, that is, the two examinations of the present day with the two examinations of the previous day and see if there is any improvement from one day to the next.

[30] 4. For the fourth direction, compare one week with another and see if the present week is an improvement on the previous week.

[31] *Note:* The first two lines represent Sunday, the second two Monday, the third two Tuesday, etc.

S _____
   _____
M _____
   _____
T _____
   _____
W _____
   _____
T _____
   _____
F _____
   _____
S _____
   _____

[32] GENERAL EXAMINATION OF CONSCIENCE

The purpose of this examination of conscience is to purify the soul and to help us to improve our confessions.

I presuppose that there are three kinds of thoughts in me. There is my own which arises entirely from my own freedom and desires. The other two come from outside, one from the good spirit and the other from the evil spirit.

[33] THOUGHTS

1. There are two ways of gaining merit from an evil thought that comes from outside. For example, there comes to my mind a thought about committing a mortal sin, which I promptly resist and overcome.

[34] 2. When the same evil thought comes to me and I resist it, but it returns again and again and I continue resisting until it is defeated. This second way is more meritorious than the first.

[35] A venial sin is committed if the same thought of committing a mortal sin suggests itself to the mind and you listen to it for a little while or receive some sensual pleasure from it, or if you are some-what negligent in banning the thought immediately.

[36] There are two ways of sinning mortally: the first is when you consent to an evil thought with the intention of acting on it later or with the desire of doing so if you can.

[37] The second way of sinning mortally is when the sin is actually carried out. This is a greater sin for three reasons: first, because it lasts longer, secondly because it is more intense and thirdly because it does greater damage to both the parties.

[38] WORDS

You must not swear either by the Creator or by the creature, unless you do so with truth, necessity and reverence. By necessity I do not mean you need to swear to state any truth, but when it is important for the benefit of soul or body or for the protection of temporal goods. By reverence I mean that when you name your Creator and Lord you should accord him due honour and reverence.

[39] In the case of a needless oath we sin more when we swear by the Creator than when we swear by the creature. It is more difficult to swear rightly, that is, with truth, necessity and reverence by the creature than by the Creator for the following reasons:

1. When we wish to swear by some creature the wish to name the creature does not make us as attentive or careful to speak the truth or to be sure it is necessary to swear as when we wish to name the Lord and Creator of all things.

2. In swearing by the creature it is not so easy to reverence and respect the Creator as when we swear by naming the Creator and Lord himself. Because the wish to name God our Lord brings with it more respect and reverence than the wish to name a created thing. Therefore it is more permissible for the perfect person to swear by the creature than for the imperfect, because the perfect by constant contemplation and the enlightenment of their understanding are more able to consider, meditate and contemplate the truth that God our Lord is in every creature by his own essence, presence and power. Thus in swearing by the creature the perfect person is more apt to show respect and reverence for his Creator and Lord than the imperfect.

3. By frequently swearing by the creature, idolatry is more to be feared in the imperfect than in the perfect.

[40] Do not speak idle words. By this I mean words that do not benefit yourself or anyone else and are not intended to do so. Speaking for the benefit or with the intention of benefiting your own soul or someone else's, for the benefit of the body or temporal goods is not idle. Even if you speak about things outside your competence, such as when a monk speaks about war or trade, in all that is said there is merit if it is spoken for a good purpose and sin if it is spoken to bad effect or idly.

[41] Do not say anything that would shame or slander another person, because if I make known a mortal sin which is not public, I myself sin mortally. If I make known a venial sin, I sin venially; and if I reveal a defect in somebody else I show a defect myself. But if the intention is wholesome, I can mention another's sin or fault in two ways:

1. It can be spoken about when the sin is public, as in the case of a public prostitute, or a sentence passed by a court of law or a public error which contaminates the souls it comes into contact with.

2. When a secret sin is made known to someone in order that that person may help the sinner to recover from the sin. In this case there must be good grounds or a reasonable expectation that help can be given.

[42] DEEDS

The subject matter here will be the ten commandments, the laws of the Church and recommendations by superiors. Anything that goes against any of these three is a greater or lesser sin according to its greater or lesser importance. By things recommended by superiors I mean papal bulls for crusades and other indulgences such as those for peace. These are to be obtained by confessing and receiving holy communion, for it is no small sin to oppose or cause others to oppose such pious exhortations and recommendations of our superiors.

[43] METHOD OF MAKING THE GENERAL EXAMINATION OF CONSCIENCE

It contains five points.

The first point is to give thanks to God our Lord for the favours we have received.

The second point is to ask for grace to know our sins and to free ourselves from them.

The third point is to demand an account of the soul: hour by hour or period by period from the time of getting up until this present examination. First the examination of thoughts, then of words, then of deeds, in the same order as that given for the particular examination of conscience.

The fourth point is to ask God our Lord to forgive our faults.

The fifth point is to resolve upon amendment with the help of God's grace. Close with an *Our Father*.

[44] GENERAL CONFESSION AND HOLY COMMUNION

The three main advantages of a general confession made voluntarily during the Spiritual Exercises are:

1. One who confesses every year is not obliged to make a general confession. But if you make one you will obtain more benefit and merit because of your great present sorrow for all the sins and wickedness of your life.

2. Since during the spiritual exercises we gain a more intimate knowledge of our sins and their wickedness than when we are not concentrating on inner matters, this increased awareness and sorrow will gain us more benefit and merit than from former confessions.

3. As we have made a better confession and are better disposed, we will find ourselves more worthy and better prepared to receive holy communion. Receiving it not only helps us not to fall into sin but also to remain in a state of grace and increase it. It is best to make this general confession immediately after the exercises of the first week.

[45] FIRST EXERCISE

The first exercise is to meditate with the three powers of the soul on the first, second and third sin. It contains a preparatory prayer, two preludes, three principal points and a colloquy.

[46] *Preparatory prayer.* The preparatory prayer is to ask God our Lord for grace to order all my intentions, gestures and actions purely in the service and praise of His Divine Majesty.

[47] *First prelude.* In the first prelude we imagine seeing the place where what we are about to meditate on occurs. We should note here

that in the contemplation or meditation on a visible object, such as contemplating Christ our Lord, who is visible, the representation will consist in seeing with the eye of the imagination the physical place where the object I wish to contemplate is. I say physical place, such as the temple or the mountain where Jesus Christ is or Our Lady is, depending on what I decide to contemplate. When the subject is invisible, as here in a meditation on sin, the representation will be to see in imagination my soul imprisoned in this corruptible body and to consider my whole self, soul and body, as an exile on earth.

[48] *Second prelude.* The second prelude is to ask God our Lord for what I want and desire. My petition should be appropriate to the subject matter. For example, if the contemplation is on the resurrection, I will ask for joy with the joyful Christ. If it is on the passion, I will ask for sorrow, tears and anguish with Christ in anguish. Here it is appropriate to ask for shame and remorse considering how many people have been lost because of a single mortal sin, and how often I have deserved eternal damnation because of the many grievous sins that I have committed.

[49] *Note.* The preparatory prayer, which is always the same, and the two preludes above, which are sometimes changed according to the subject matter, must always be made before all the contemplations and meditations.

[50] *First point.* The first point will consist in recalling the first sin, which was that of the angels. Then I should apply my mind to it and then my will, wanting all this remembering and understanding to make me more ashamed and remorseful. I should compare the angels' one sin with so many sins of mine. They were sent to hell for one sin; how often I have deserved this for so many sins. I say call to memory the angels' sin, who were created in grace and did not want to use their freedom to reverence and obey their Creator and Lord. They became proud and turned from grace to wickedness and were thrown out of heaven into hell. Ponder this in your mind so that your feelings are moved by your will.

[51] *Second point.* The second point is to do likewise, bringing the three powers of the soul to bear upon the sin of Adam and Eve. Consider how for this sin they did such long penance, how much corruption came into the human race, and how many people went to hell. I say you must call to memory the second sin, that of our first

parents. Remember how after Adam was created on the plain of Damascus and placed in the earthly paradise, and Eve was created from his rib, they were forbidden to eat from the tree of knowledge. But they did eat and thereby sinned. Then clothed in garments of skin they were thrown out of paradise and spent their whole lives in toil and penance. You should ponder this carefully in your mind and use the will as before.

[52] *Third point.* The third point is to do the same with the third sin. This is the particular sin of anyone who through one mortal sin has gone to hell. Countless others have gone to hell for fewer sins than I have committed. So do the same for this third sin, remembering the gravity and wickedness of sin against our Creator and Lord. Ponder in your mind how in sinning and going against the Infinite Goodness the sinner has justly been condemned for ever. End with the acts of the will as before.

[53] *Colloquy.* Imagine Christ our Lord before you on the cross, converse with him about how from being the Creator he became man and from eternal life he came to death in time and died for our sins. I shall also reflect on myself and what I have done for Christ, what I am doing for Christ and what I should do for Christ. Seeing him hanging on the cross, I shall ponder upon whatever it might suggest to my mind.

[54] The colloquy should be like a conversation between friends or between servant and master. We should sometimes ask for some grace, sometimes blame ourselves for some wrong we have done, sometimes discuss our own affairs and ask for advice. End with an *Our Father.*

[55] SECOND EXERCISE
   Here we meditate on our sins. First there is the preparatory prayer; then the two preludes, then five points and a colloquy.

Prayer. The preparatory prayer is the same.

First prelude. The first prelude is the same as in the first exercise.

Second prelude. This is to ask for what I desire. Here I should ask for increased intense sorrow and tears for my sins.

[56] *First point.* The first point is to review my sins. I will recall all the sins of my life, from year to year or period to period. Three things are helpful in this: first, to see the place and house where I have lived; second, the dealings I have had with others; third, the work I have done.

[57] *Second point.* The second point is to examine my sins, considering the ugliness and wickedness that each mortal sin committed has in itself, even were it not forbidden.

[58] *Third point.* The third point is to consider who I am, humbling myself through the following comparisons. Firstly, what am I in comparison with all other human beings? Secondly, what are human beings in comparison with all the angels and saints in heaven? Thirdly, what is all creation compared to God? So on my own, what am I? Fourthly, I will reflect on the corruption and loathsomeness of my body. Fifthly, I will regard myself as a source of corruption and contagion from which so many sins and evils have issued.

[59] *Fourth point.* The fourth point is to consider who God is, against whom I have sinned. Contemplate his attributes and compare them with their opposites in myself. Compare his wisdom with my ignorance, his omnipotence with my weakness, his justice with my wickedness, his goodness with my evil.

[60] *Fifth point.* The fifth point is an exclamation of wonder. With growing delight I let my mind wander over all creatures, and how they have enabled me to live and stay alive. Think of the angels, who are the sword of divine justice, how they have tolerated me, guarded me and prayed for me. Think of the saints, how they have interceded and prayed for me, and the sky, sun, moon, stars, elements, fruits, birds, fishes and animals. Think how the earth has not opened up and swallowed me, creating new hells in which I should suffer for ever.

[61] *Colloquy.* I will conclude with a colloquy on mercy. I will thank God our Lord that he has kept me alive until now. I will resolve with his grace to amend my life in future. End with an *Our Father.*

[62] THIRD EXERCISE
The third exercise is a repetition of the first and second exercises with three colloquies.

After the preparatory prayer and the two preludes, repeat the first and second exercises. Note and dwell on the points where I have felt great consolation or desolation or greater spiritual feeling. After that I make three colloquies as follows.

[63] *First colloquy.* The first colloquy is with Our Lady that she may obtain grace for me from her Son and Lord for three things. The first is that I may have a deep knowledge of my sins and abhorrence of them. The second is that I may feel the disorder of my actions, so that I can abhor them and amend my life and bring order into it. The third is to ask for knowledge of the world, so that I may abhor it and set aside worldly and frivolous things. Then I will say a *Hail Mary.*

Second colloquy. In the second colloquy I will make the same petitions to the Son, so that he may obtain these graces for me from the Father. Finish with the *Anima Christi.*

Third colloquy. I will make the same requests to the Father, so that he himself, the eternal Lord, may grant them to me. Then I will end with an *Our Father.*

[64] FOURTH EXERCISE

The fourth exercise is a summary of the third. I say summary meaning that the mind should assiduously go over the things contemplated before. The same three colloquies should be used at the end of this exercise.

[65] FIFTH EXERCISE

This is a meditation on hell. It contains the preparatory prayer and two preludes, then five points and a colloquy.

Prayer. The preparatory prayer is the same as before.

First prelude. The first prelude is a representation of the place. Here it means seeing with the imagination the length, breadth and depth of hell.

Second prelude. The second prelude is to ask for what I desire. Here it is to ask for a deep sense of the pain suffered by the damned. I ask this so that if through my faults I should forget the love of the eternal Lord, at least the fear of these pains will help me not to fall into sin.

[66] *First point*. This will be to see in imagination the vast fires and the souls as if trapped in bodies on fire.

[67] *Second point*. Hear the screams, howls, cries, blasphemies against Christ our Lord and all his saints.

[68] *Third point*. Smell the smoke, sulphur, filth and decomposition.

[69] *Fourth point*. Taste the bitterness, tears, sadness and remorse.

[70] *Fifth point*. Feel with your sense of touch how the fires envelop and burn the souls.

[71] *Colloquy*. Converse with Christ our Lord, remembering the souls who are in hell, some because they did not believe in his coming, others because despite their belief they disobeyed his commandments. These people fall into three groups. The first are those who were lost before his coming, the second those who were lost during his life on earth, the third those who were lost after Christ's life in this world. Then I will thank God because he has not let me fall into any of these groups by ending my life. I shall also thank God for treating me with such pity and mercy. Finish with an *Our Father*.

[72] *Note*. The first exercise should be done at midnight. The second on rising in the morning, the third before or after Mass, as long as it is before lunch. The fourth should be done at the hour of Vespers, the fifth an hour before supper. This arrangement of hours should be followed more or less throughout the four weeks. This depends on whether the age, temperament and health of the person on retreat allow for the doing of five exercises or fewer.

[73] ADDITIONAL DIRECTIONS

These directions are intended to help the retreatants to do the exercises better and find more readily what they seek.

1. At night before falling asleep, for the space of a *Hail Mary* I will think of the time when I have to rise and why, and will briefly review the exercise to be done.

[74] 2. When I wake up, before thinking about anything else, I will think about what I am going to contemplate in the first exercise at

midnight. I will try to be ashamed of my many sins, with examples. Like a knight standing before the king and his whole court, ashamed and dismayed because he has greatly offended one from whom he had previously received many gifts and favours. Likewise in the second exercise I will think of myself as a great sinner. I am led in chains before the supreme and eternal judge. I will imagine prisoners in chains who deserve death appearing before their earthly judge. While getting dressed I will ponder these thoughts or others appropriate to the subject matter of the meditation.

[75] 3. I will stand a step or two from the place where I am to contemplate or meditate. For the space of an *Our Father,* with my mind recollected, I shall consider how God our Lord sees me. Then I will make an act of reverence or humility.

[76] 4. The fourth direction concerns my posture at prayer as I start contemplation. I must discover the posture most conducive to prayer, whether it be kneeling, prostrate on the ground, lying face upwards, sitting, standing. Here we shall add two observations. The first is that if I find kneeling conducive, I should stay that way. Likewise with lying flat or any other posture. The second is that when I find a particular point in the meditation gives me what I am looking for, I should stay with it, without being anxious to move on until I am ready.

[77] 5. After finishing the exercise, for a quarter of an hour, either sitting or strolling, I will reflect on how the contemplation or meditation has gone for me. If it has gone badly I will look for the cause and when I have discovered it I will repent so that I can amend it in future. If it has gone well, I shall thank God our Lord and continue in the same way next time.

[78] 6. I should not think of pleasant and happy things like glory, the resurrection etc. For any consideration of joy and delight hinders the feeling of sorrow, pain and tears for my sins. I will concentrate on wanting to feel sorrow and pain for my sins. It would therefore be better to think of death and judgement.

[79] 7. Here the object is the same as that of the sixth. I deprive myself of all light, closing the shutters and doors in my room.

[80] 8. I must not laugh or say anything to cause laughter.

[81] 9. This deals with the control of the eyes. I should only look at people when I greet them or say goodbye.

[82] 10. The tenth is about penance, which is divided into interior and exterior. Interior penance is to grieve for your sins with a firm intention never again to commit them or any others. Exterior penance is the fruit of the former. It consists in inflicting punishment on ourselves for sins committed. There are three principal ways of doing exterior penance.

[83] *First way.* This has to do with eating. When we do without what is superfluous this is not penance but moderation. Penance is when we do without what is reasonable. The more we do without, the greater and better the penance, as long as we do not damage ourselves or cause ill health.

[84] *Second way.* This concerns sleeping. It is not a penance to do without a superfluity of pleasant things, but it is a penance to do without what we need, and the more we do so the better the penance, as long as we do not damage ourselves or cause ill health. We should not do without sleep we really need unless we have a slothful habit of sleeping too much, but we must be reasonable.

[85] *Third way.* The third way is to chastise our body. Make it feel pain by wearing a hair shirt or cords or iron chains next to the skin, or by whipping or wounding it or through other austerities.

[86] What seems most appropriate and safe in penance is that the pain is felt by the body but the bones remain unaffected. It should inflict pain but not cause illness. So it seems better to scourge yourself with thin cords, which cause superficial pain but do not cause serious internal damage.

[87] *First note.* Exterior penance is done chiefly for three purposes: first to make satisfaction for former sins; second, to conquer ourselves, that is, to make sensuality obey reason and to subject all our inferior faculties to our higher ones; third, to seek and receive some grace or gift that we want or desire. For example, we may want to have inner contrition for our sins or to weep much over them or over the pains and sorrows that Christ our Lord suffered in his passion. Or we may want to solve some doubt in our mind.

[88] *Second note.* The first and second additional directions are to be observed for the exercises at midnight and dawn and not for exercises done at other times. The fourth direction is never to be followed in church in front of others, but in secret, at home.

[89] *Third note.* When you do not find what you seek, for example, tears, consolations etc., it is often helpful to change your eating or sleeping habits or other ways of doing penance. For example, we can spend two or three days doing penance and desist for the next two or three days. Some people find it helpful to do penance frequently, others achieve the same doing it less frequently. We often fail to do penance through self indulgence and through a mistaken judgement that a human being cannot bear the penance without getting ill. On the other hand sometimes we do too much, thinking that our body can stand it. God our Lord knows our constitution infinitely better than we do. He often helps us to know which of these penances is suited to us personally.

[90] *Fourth note.* The particular examination of conscience should be directed to getting rid of faults and negligences in the practice of the Exercises and the additional directions. The same procedure should be followed for the second, third and fourth weeks.

Second week

[91] THE CALL OF AN EARTHLY KING
This will aid us to contemplate the life of the eternal King.

Prayer. The preparatory prayer is the usual one.

First prelude. The first prelude is to imagine the place. Look with the eyes of the imagination at the synagogues, towns and villages where Christ our Lord preached.

Second prelude. The second prelude is to ask for the grace I desire. Here it will be to ask our Lord for the grace not to be deaf to his call, but to be eager and willing to carry out his most holy will.

[92] FIRST PART

First point. Imagine an earthly king, chosen by God our Lord. All Christian princes and people respect and obey him.

[93] *Second point.* See how this king speaks to his people saying: 'My will is to conquer all the land of the heathen. So whoever wants to come with me must be willing to eat, drink and dress like me. Likewise he must work with me by day and watch with me by night. Then he will share in the victory with me as he has shared in the labour with me'.

[94] *Third point.* Consider how loyal subjects should answer such a generous and gracious king. So if anyone did not accept the summons of such a king he would deserve to be scorned by the whole world as an unworthy subject.

[95] SECOND PART

In the second part of the exercise apply the above example of an earthly king to Christ our Lord, point by point.

First point. If we listen to the earthly king's call to his subjects, how much more worthy of hearing is Christ our Lord, the eternal king over the whole world. He calls each one of us in particular and says: 'My will is to conquer the whole world and all my enemies, and thereby enter into my Father's glory. So anyone who wants to come with me must work with me, so that by following me in suffering he may follow me in glory.'

[96] *Second point.* Consider that all who have judgement and reason will offer themselves entirely for this work.

[97] *Third point.* Those who wish to show more affection and distinguish themselves in entire devotion to their eternal king and universal lord will not only offer themselves entirely for the work but, by going against their own ease and natural and worldly inclinations, they will also make offerings of greater worth and importance. They will say:

[98] *Eternal Lord of all things, I make my offering with your favour and help in the presence of your infinite goodness and of your glorious mother and all the saints, men and women, in your heavenly court. I want and desire and it is my determined resolve (providing that this is to your greater service and praise) to imitate you in bearing all injuries and insults and all poverty, both physical and spiritual, if your most holy majesty wishes to choose and receive me into such a life and state.*

[99] *First note.* This exercise is to be done twice a day, that is, in the morning upon getting up and an hour before lunch or supper.

[100]*Second note.* During the second week and thereafter, it would be very helpful to read a little from the *Imitation of Christ* or the Gospels and the lives of the saints.

[101] FIRST DAY AND FIRST CONTEMPLATION

This is a contemplation on the incarnation. It contains the preparatory prayer, three preludes, three points and a colloquy.

Prayer. The usual preparatory prayer.

[102] *First prelude.* The first prelude is to call to mind the background of the subject I have to contemplate. Here it will be the Three Divine Persons looking down on the whole expanse of the earth and all the people inhabiting it. Seeing that they were all going down into hell, the Trinity resolved in their eternal wisdom that the Second Person should become man to save the human race. In the fullness of time the angel Gabriel was sent to Our Lady. See [262].

[103] *Second prelude.* A mental representation of the place. Here we should see the vastness of the world in which so many and various peoples live. Then we should imagine Our Lady's house and rooms in the town of Nazareth in the province of Galilee.

[104] *Third prelude.* The third prelude is to ask for what I desire. Here I should ask for a deep knowledge of Our Lord, who became man for me, so that I may love him more and follow him more closely.

[105] *Note.* We should note here that the same preparatory prayer, without change, as we said at the beginning, and the same three preludes are to be made during this week and the subsequent ones, changing the form according to the subject matter.

[106] *First point.* See all the different people. *Firstly,* all the people on the face of the earth, in all their variety of dress and behaviour, some white, some black, some in peace, others at war, some weeping and others laughing, some healthy and others sick, some being born and others dying.

Secondly, see and consider the Three Divine Persons as on their royal seat or throne of their divine majesty. They look down on the whole earth and all the people in their blindness, dying and going down into hell.

Thirdly, see Our Lady, and the angel greeting her, and reflect in order to derive profit from this sight.

[107] *Second point.* Hear what the people on the face of the earth are saying. Hear how they speak to one another, how they swear and blaspheme etc. Likewise listen to what the Divine Persons are saying,

'Let us redeem the human race' etc. Then listen to what the angel and Our Lady say, and reflect in order to benefit from their words.

[108] *Third point.* See what the people on the face of the earth are doing: wounding, killing, and going to hell etc. Likewise, look at what the Divine Persons are doing, that is, bringing about the holy incarnation etc. Likewise what the angel and Our Lady are doing, that is, the angel is doing his work as messenger and Our Lady is humbling herself and giving thanks to the Divine Majesty. Then reflect in order to derive profit from each of these details.

[109] *Colloquy.* Finally make a colloquy. I will think over what I should say to the Three Divine Persons or to the eternal Word incarnate or to his Mother, Our Lady. According to the light I have received, I will ask for grace to follow and imitate more closely Our Lord, who has just become man for me. Finish with an *Our Father*.

[110] SECOND CONTEMPLATION
The second contemplation is on the nativity.

Prayer. The usual preparatory prayer.

[111] *First prelude.* The history of the mystery. Here, think how they set out from Nazareth. Our Lady nearly nine months pregnant and, as we may reverently imagine, riding on a donkey, and Joseph and a servant girl leading an ox to Bethlehem, to pay the tax that Caesar demanded from all those territories. See [264].

[112] *Second prelude.* The mental representation of the place. In this case it will be to imagine the road from Nazareth to Bethlehem. Consider its length, breadth, whether it is level, whether it goes uphill or downhill. Likewise look at the place or cave where the birth took place, how large or small it is, how high or low, and how it was furnished.

[113] *Third prelude.* The third prelude is the same as in the preceding contemplation.

[114] *First point.* See the people, that is, Our Lady and Joseph and the servant girl and the child Jesus, after he is born. I imagine myself a poor unworthy little slave, watching them, contemplating them and

serving their needs, as if I was present there, with the utmost respect and reverence. Then I reflect upon myself to derive some benefit.

[115] *Second point.* Look, notice and contemplate what they are saying. Then reflect upon myself and draw some profit from it.

[116] *Third point.* Look and consider what they are doing. For example, their journey and their labour, the Lord being born in extreme poverty, and after so many hardships, hunger, thirst, heat and cold, insults and injuries, dying on the cross. He did all this for me. Then I reflect to derive some spiritual benefit from what I have seen.

[117] *Colloquy.* Close with a colloquy, as in the previous contemplation and the *Our Father.*

[118] THIRD CONTEMPLATION
This will be a repetition of the first and second exercises.

After the preparatory prayer and the three preludes, repeat the first and second exercises. Always note some of the chief parts where you have felt some insight, consolation or desolation. Likewise make a colloquy at the end and close with an *Our Father.*

[119] In this repetition and in all those that follow do everything in the same order as in the repetitions of the first week, altering the subject matter but keeping to the same method.

[120] FOURTH CONTEMPLATION
The fourth contemplation is a repetition of the first and second exercises in the same way as in the repetition above.

[121] FIFTH CONTEMPLATION
The fifth contemplation consists in applying the five senses to the subject matter of the first and second contemplations.

Prayer. After the preparatory prayer and the three preludes it is helpful to apply the five senses of the imagination to the first and second contemplations in the following manner:

[122] *First point*. See the people with the eye of the imagination, meditating and contemplating especially on their circumstances, and deriving some benefit from what has been seen.

[123] *Second point*. Listen with your hearing to what they are saying or might say. Reflect on this to derive some profit from what has been said.

[124] *Third point*. Smell the infinite fragrance and taste the infinite sweetness of the divinity. Apply the same senses to the soul, its virtues and to everything else, according to the person contemplated. Then reflect on yourself and draw some benefit from it.

[125] *Fourth point*. This is to apply the sense of touch. For example, embrace and kiss the places where the people contemplated, walked or sat, always trying to derive some profit from it.

[126] *Colloquy*. End with a colloquy, and an *Our Father* as in the first and second contemplation.

[127] *First note*. Throughout this and the following weeks I am only to read the mystery I am about to contemplate. For the moment I should not read any mystery which I am not to meditate on that day or that hour, so that the consideration of one mystery does not disturb the consideration of the other.

[128] *Second note*. The first exercise on the incarnation is to be done at midnight; the second at daybreak; the third at the time of the Mass; the fourth at the hour of Vespers, and the fifth before supper. Each exercise should take an hour. The same order is to be observed on all following days.

[129] *Third note*. If the person doing the exercises is old or frail or, even though in robust health, has become exhausted from the first week, it would be better if, at least sometimes, he or she does not get up at midnight, but do one contemplation in the early morning, another at the time for Mass, and another before lunch. Then do one repetition of these at the time of Vespers, followed by the application of the senses before supper.

[130] *Fourth note.* Of the ten additional directions given in the first week, the second, sixth, seventh and part of the tenth should be changed in the second week.

For the second direction is that, as soon as I wake up, I should set before my mind the subject of the contemplation I am to do, with the desire to know better the eternal Word incarnate, so that I can serve him and follow him more closely.

The sixth direction will be frequently to call to mind the life and mysteries of Christ our Lord, beginning with his incarnation until the place or mystery I am engaged in contemplating.

The seventh will be to take care to use darkness or light, good or bad weather, for whatever you feel will benefit and help you find what you want are seeking to attain through the exercises.

In the tenth direction the retreatant should behave in accordance with the mysteries contemplated. For some of them require penance and others do not. So be sure to employ the ten directions with great care.

[131] *Fifth note.* In all the exercises, except the midnight and early morning ones, adopt the equivalent of the second direction in the following manner. As soon as I remember it is time for the exercise I am to do, before going to it, I should remind myself where I am going and into whose presence, and briefly review the exercise. Then I follow the third direction and start the exercise.

[132] *Second day.* For the first and second contemplations take the presentation in the temple [268]   and the flight into Egypt [269]. With these two contemplations do two repetitions and apply the five senses to them in the same way as on the day before.

[133] *Note.* Even if the retreatant is strong and well, sometimes it is appropriate to make some of the following changes. From this second day to the fourth day inclusive, in order to say what you want more readily, do only one contemplation at daybreak, another about the hour of Mass and repeat them at the hour of Vespers and the application of the senses before supper.

[134] *Third day.* Reflect on how the Child Jesus was obedient to his parents in Nazareth [271] and how they afterwards found him in the temple [272]. Then do the two repetitions and the application of the five senses.

[135] INTRODUCTION TO THE CONSIDERATION OF DIFFERENT STATES OF LIFE

We have already considered the example which Christ our Lord gave of the first state, keeping the commandments and obeying his parents. Likewise for the second state of evangelical perfection, when he remained in the temple, leaving his adoptive father and natural mother, in order to be free to serve only his eternal Father. As we contemplate his life, we shall also be trying to discover in what kind of life or state he wishes to make use of us. And so, by way of an introduction to this matter, in the first exercise that follows we shall see Christ our Lord's intention and, on the other hand, that of the enemy of human nature. We discover how we ought to behave in order to become perfect in whatever state of life God our Lord may grant us to choose.

[136] *Fourth day.* Meditation on the two standards. One is of Christ, our supreme leader and lord. The other is of Lucifer, the mortal enemy of our human nature.

Prayer. The usual preparatory prayer.

[137] *First prelude.* The first prelude is the history. Here it is how Christ calls us and wants all of us to come under his standard. How Lucifer opposes this and wants everyone to come under his.

[138] *Second prelude.* The second prelude is to imagine the place. Here it will be a great plain covering the whole region of Jerusalem, where the supreme commander of the good is Christ our Lord. On another plain in the region of Babylon the leader of the enemy is Lucifer.

[139] *Third prelude.* The third prelude is to ask for what I desire. Here it will be to ask for awareness of the tricks of the wicked leader and help to guard myself against them. I ask for knowledge of the true life as shown by our supreme and true commander, and grace to imitate him.

[140] *First point.* Imagine how the enemy leader takes up his position on that great plain of Babylon, as if on a great throne of fire and smoke, a hideous and terrifying sight.

[141] *Second point.* See him calling together innumerable demons, and how he disposes of these troops, some to one city and some to another, throughout the whole world. He does not leave uncovered any province, place, state of life or individual.

[142] *Third point.* Consider the speech he makes to them and how he urges them to set traps and snares. First they are to tempt people with greed for riches (as he does in most cases) so that they may easily be caught up in the vain honour of the world, and overweening pride. Thus the first downward step is riches, the second honour and the third pride. By these three steps he leads us into all other vices.

[143] On the other hand we should imagine our supreme and true commander, who is Christ our Lord.

[144] *First point.* Consider how Christ our Lord takes his stand on the great plain in the region of Jerusalem, in a humble place. His aspect is beautiful and gracious.

[145] *Second point.* Think how the Lord of the whole world chooses so many people, apostles, disciples etc. and sends them throughout the whole world, spreading his holy teaching among all kinds of people.

[146] *Third point.* Hear the speech that Christ our Lord makes to all his servants and friends, whom he sends on this expedition, telling them to try to help all people. First they are to attract people to perfect spiritual poverty and, if the Divine Majesty pleases and wishes to choose them, to actual poverty as well. Secondly, they should lead people to desire insults and contempt, because these give rise to humility. Thus there are three steps: first, poverty against wealth; second, insults or belittlement against worldly honour; third, humility against pride. These three steps may lead on to all the other virtues.

[147] *First colloquy.* A conversation with Our Lady, to obtain grace for me from her Son and Lord, that I may be accepted under his standard. First, that I may attain perfect spiritual poverty, and if the Divine Majesty pleases and wishes to choose me and receive me, actual poverty too. Second, that I may suffer insults and injuries in order to imitate him better in these. But let these happen without anyone sinning or any displeasure to God. End with a *Hail Mary.*

Second colloquy. This will be to ask her Son to obtain the same grace for me from the Father. Then I will say the *Anima Christi*.

Third colloquy. I ask the Father the same graces. Then I will say the *Our Father*.

[148] *Note*. This exercise is to be done at midnight and then again in the morning. Two repetitions of it are to be made at the hour of Mass and the hour of Vespers, always ending with the three colloquies with Our Lady, with her Son and with the Father. The meditation on the three classes of people that follows is to be done during the hour before supper.

[149] *Quarto giomo*. On the same fourth day do the meditation on the three classes of people, in order to choose the best.

   Prayer. The usual preparatory prayer.

[150] *First prelude*. The first prelude is the history of the three classes of people. Each of them has acquired ten thousand ducats, not purely and properly for the love of God. They all want to be saved and find peace in God our Lord, by ridding themselves of the weight and impediment, with which their attachment to their possessions burdens them.

[151] *Second prelude*. I form a picture of the place. Here it will be to see myself, as I stand before God our Lord and all his saints, so that I may desire and know what is most pleasing to him.

[152] *Third prelude*. Here I ask for what I desire: the grace to choose what is more to the glory of the Divine Majesty and the salvation of my soul.

[153] *The first class*. The first class of people wish to get rid of the attachment they have to their possessions, to find peace in God our Lord, and be able to be saved. Right up to the hour of death they do not avail themselves of the means of achieving this.

[154] *The second class*. They wish to be rid of their attachment, but in such a way that they hang on to the possessions they have acquired.

They want to decide where God comes in and are not prepared to leave their possessions to go to God, even though this might be the better state for them.

[155] *The third class.* These people want to get rid of their attachment, but they want to do so in such a way that they no longer care whether they have the thing they have acquired or not. They only seek to will it or not will it according to the plan of God our Lord, or according to whether it appears better for the service and praise of the Divine Majesty. Meanwhile they do let go of their attachment, and strive not to want anything whatever unless it is for the service of God our Lord. Thus the desire to be able to serve God our Lord better is what moves them to accept or reject anything.

[156] *Three colloquies.* Make the same three colloquies as were made in the preceding contemplation on the two standards [147].

[157] *Note.* When we feel an attachment which is opposed to poverty, when we are not indifferent to poverty or wealth, a great help towards severing such a disordered attachment is to ask in the colloquies (even though it goes against our feelings) that the Lord should choose us to serve him in actual poverty. Seek it and earnestly ask for it so long as it is for the service and praise of God.

[158] *Fifth day.* Contemplation on the journey of Christ our Lord from Nazareth to the River Jordan, and his baptism [273].

[159] *First note.* This contemplation is to be done once at midnight and again in the morning, with two repetitions of it at the hour of Mass and Vespers. Before supper there will be the application of the senses to the subject matter. In each of these five exercises there will be the usual preparatory prayer and the three preludes just as in the contemplation of the incarnation and the nativity. Conclude with the three colloquies on the three classes or follow the note that appears at the end of that meditation.

[160] *Second note.* The particular examination of conscience after lunch and supper will be on the faults and negligences in the practice of the exercises and additional directions of this day. The same will be observed on the subsequent days.

[161] *Sixth day*. Contemplation of how Christ our Lord went from the River Jordan into the wilderness, and how he was tempted there. The same directions that were given for the fifth day will be followed here.

Seventh day. How St Andrew and others followed Christ our Lord [275].

Eighth day. The eight beatitudes from the Sermon on the Mount [278].

Ninth day. How our Lord appeared to his disciples on the waves of the sea [279].

Tenth day. How the Lord preached in the temple [288].

Eleventh day. The raising of Lazarus [285].

Twelfth day. Palm Sunday [287].

[162] *First note*. The contemplations for this second week can be lengthened or shortened according to the wishes and needs of the person doing the exercises. If you want to lengthen them you can take the mysteries of the visitation of Our Lady to St Elizabeth, the shepherds, the circumcision of the Child Jesus, the three kings and other subjects. If you want to shorten them, you can even omit some of those listed above because this is intended only as an introduction and method to contemplate better and more fully later.

[163] *Second note*. The material for the choice of a way of life will begin from the contemplation of Christ's departure from Nazareth to the Jordan, until the fifth day, as is explained below.

[164] *Third note*. Before beginning the choice it is very helpful to consider the following three kinds of humility, thinking about them occasionally during the day, and also making the colloquies as indicated below. This will help us feel attached to the true teaching of Christ our Lord.

[165] *First kind of humility*. The first kind of humility is necessary for eternal salvation. It is to abase and humble myself as much as I can, so that in all things I obey the law of God our Lord. This would

mean that even were I made lord of all created things in this world, I would not even think of breaking a divine or human commandment, even to save my physical life, because this would lead me into mortal sin.

[166] *Second kind of humility.* This is more perfect than the first. It means not wanting or preferring riches to poverty, honour to dishonour, a long life to a short one, as long as either is equally advantageous to the service of God and the salvation of my soul. Furthermore I would not think of committing a venial sin for any created thing or even to save my life.

[167] *Third kind of humility.* The third kind is the most perfect humility. This includes the first and second kinds as long as the praise and glory of the Divine Majesty is equally served. In order to imitate and become more really like Christ our Lord, I want and choose poverty with Christ who was poor rather than wealth, insults with Christ who was abused with them, rather than honour. I must prefer to be thought of as worthless and a fool for Christ, rather than to be esteemed as wise and prudent in this world.

[168] *Note.* If we wish to attain this third kind of humility it is very helpful to make the three colloquies about the classes of people, asking our Lord to deign to choose us for this third greatest and best kind of humility, so that we may imitate and serve him better as long as this will be to the greater service and praise of the Divine Majesty.

[169] INTRODUCTION TO MAKING THE CHOICE OF A WAY OF LIFE

In any good choice, insofar as it depends on us, our intention must be single-minded. I must focus exclusively on what I am created for, that is, the praise of God our Lord and the salvation of my soul. Therefore anything I choose must be to help me to achieve the end for which I was created.

I must not adapt the end to the means but the means to the end. For example, it happens that many people choose first to marry, which is a means, and secondly to serve God our Lord in marriage, whereas serving God is the end. Likewise there are others who want to have a certain job and then serve God in it. Thus these people do not go straight to God, but want God to come straight to their disordered affections. They turn the end into a means and the means into the end. So they make what should be primary become secondary.

Our first object must be to want to serve God, who is the end, and marrying or having a job should be secondary, according to what suits me as a means to the end. Therefore nothing should induce me to use these means or do without them except the service and praise of God our Lord and the eternal salvation of my soul.

[170] CONSIDERATION
The purpose of this consideration is to provide guidance on the matters about which a choice has to be made. There are four points and a note.

First point. It is necessary that all the things we wish to choose from should be either indifferent or good in themselves. They must be lawful within our Holy Mother the Church and must not be damaging or opposed to her.

[171] *Second point.* There are some things which require a permanent choice, such as the priesthood, marriage etc. There are other things that admit a choice that can be changed, such as taking a job or leaving it, accepting or renouncing temporal goods.

[172] *Third point.* In choices which cannot be changed, once the choice has been made there is no more choosing to be done, because it cannot be undone. This applies to marriage, the priesthood etc. But it should be noted that if you have not made a correct choice, you can regret it, but not with disordered affections, and must try to lead a good life in the way you have chosen.

However, such a choice does not seem to be a divine vocation as it was made in a wrong and disordered way. Many people make this error, mistaking a wrong and bad choice for a divine vocation. For every divine vocation is always pure and clear and not tainted by human desires or any other disordered affection.

[173] *Fourth point.* If you make a proper and orderly choice in matters where the choice can be changed, unless you become self-indulgent and worldly, there is no reason to change the choice but it is better to perfect yourself in what you have chosen as far as you can.

[174] *Note.* When this changeable choice has not been made sincerely and correctly, then it is expedient to remake it properly, if you want it to produce results which are pleasing to God our Lord.

[175] THREE TIMES WHEN A SOUND AND GOOD CHOICE MAY BE MADE

First time. When God our Lord moves and attracts the will in such a way that, without doubting or being able to doubt, the faithful soul follows what it has been shown. This happened to St Paul and St Matthew when they followed Christ our Lord.

[176] *Second time.* When a great deal of light and insight is received through the experience of consolation and desolation, and through the experience of discernment of spirits.

[177] *Third time.* The third time is a tranquil one, when we consider what human beings are born for, that is, to praise God our Lord and save their souls. And wanting this we choose a life or state within the Church's bounds, to help us in the service of our Lord and the salvation of our soul. I call it a tranquil time because the soul is not agitated by various spirits and uses its natural powers freely and calmly.

[178] If a choice has not been made in the first or second time, there are two ways of making it during the third time.

FIRST WAY

The first way of making a sound and good choice contains six points:

First point. The first point is to set before my mind that about which I want to make a choice, such as whether to accept or refuse an office or job, or anything else about which my choice can change.

[179] *Second point.* I must have as my object the end for which I was created, which is to praise God our Lord and save my soul. Therefore I must become indifferent, without any disordered affection, so that I

am not more inclined or eager to accept rather than to refuse what is proposed, or more inclined to refuse than to accept it. I must stand as at the balancing point of a scales in order to follow what I feel will be more to the glory and praise of God our Lord and the salvation of my soul.

[180] *Third point.* I must pray God our Lord to move my will and place in my mind what I must do about the thing proposed, so that it will be more to his praise and glory. I must turn it over well and carefully in my mind and choose in accordance with his most holy will and good pleasure.

[181] *Fourth point.* I must consider the matter, weighing up the advantages and benefits that will come to me through the office or job, solely for the praise of God our Lord and the salvation of my soul. And on the other hand, I must consider the disadvantages and dangers it may lead to. Likewise I must consider the advantages and benefits in not having the office or job and on the other hand, the disadvantages and dangers in not having it.

[182] *Fifth point.* After I have considered every aspect of the proposed offer, I should judge what is the most reasonable decision, and choose on the grounds of reason not on the grounds of comfort or inclination.

[183] *Sixth point.* After the choice has been made the person who has made it must pray very earnestly to God our Lord and ask him to receive the choice and confirm it, so that it may be to his greater service and praise.

[184] SECOND WAY
   This contains four rules and a note.

First rule. The first rule is that the love which moves me and makes me choose should come down from above, from the love of God. When you choose you must feel that the greater or lesser love you have for the thing chosen is solely on account of your Creator and Lord.

[185] *Second rule.* The second rule is to look at someone I have never seen or known and want perfection for this person. I should

consider what I would tell him to do and choose for God's greater glory and the greater perfection of his soul. Then I should do likewise and follow the rule I have made for others.

[186] *Third rule.* The third rule is to imagine I am about to die. Then I should consider what choice I would want to have made then about my present dilemma. Then I should abide by that.

[187] *Fourth rule.* The fourth rule is to imagine how I shall stand on the day of judgement and consider what choice I will want to have made then about my present dilemma. What I will want to have done then, I should do now, because then I shall feel pleased and happy.

[188] *Note.* Taking into account the above rules for my salvation and eternal rest, I make my choice and offering to God our Lord, in accordance with the sixth point under the first way.

[189] METHOD FOR AMENDING AND REFORMING YOUR PRESENT LIFE AND STATE

The clergy or married people (whether rich in temporal goods or not) may not have the opportunity or may not be very willing to make a choice about things that come under changeable choices. In this case it is very helpful, instead of making the choice, to attempt to amend and reform your life and state. Your work, your life and state must be for the glory and praise of God our Lord and the salvation of your own soul.

In order to attain this end you must consider and ponder with care by doing the exercises and using the methods of choosing as already explained, to decide how large a house and household you ought to have, how you should run it and how you should teach your household by word and example. Likewise you should consider how much of your wealth you should spend on your family and household and how much you should spend on the poor and other charitable causes.

You must not want or seek anything at all but desire in everything and through everything the greater praise and glory of God our Lord. You should remember that you can only progress in spiritual matters insofar as you rid yourself of self-love, self-will and self-interest.

Third week

[190] FIRST DAY AND FIRST CONTEMPLATION

The first contemplation, at midnight, is how Christ our Lord went from Bethany to Jerusalem up to and including the Last Supper [289]. It contains the preparatory prayer, three preludes, six points and a colloquy.

Prayer. The usual preparatory prayer.

[191] *First prelude.* The first prelude calls to mind the history of how Christ our Lord sent two disciples from Bethany to Jerusalem to prepare the supper. Then he himself came there with his other disciples. After eating the paschal lamb and after having supped, he washed their feet, and gave his most sacred body and precious blood to his disciples. When Judas had gone out to sell his Lord, Christ addressed his disciples.

[192] *Second prelude.* The second prelude is to imagine the place. Consider here the road from Bethany to Jerusalem, whether it is broad or narrow, flat etc. Likewise imagine the place of the supper, whether the room was large or small, furnished this way or that.

[193] *Third prelude.* The third prelude is to ask for what I desire. Here I should ask for heartfelt sorrow and shame, because the Lord is going to his suffering for my sins.

[194] *First point.* See the people at the supper and reflect about myself so that I can derive profit from these reflections.

Second point. Hear what they are saying and likewise derive some profit from it.

Third point. Watch what they are doing and derive some profit from it.

[195] *Fourth point.* Consider what Christ our Lord suffers in his human nature or wants to suffer, according to the passage we are contemplating. I should put great effort into this and force myself to grieve, sorrow and weep. I should do the same for the other points that follow.

[196] *Fifth point.* Consider how the divinity is hidden. Even though he could destroy his enemies, he does not, and allows his most sacred humanity to suffer so cruelly.

[197] *Sixth point.* Realise how all this suffering is for my sins etc., and decide what I must do and suffer for him.

[198] *Colloquy.* End with a colloquy with Christ our Lord, and recite the *Our Father*.

[199] *Note.* As mentioned above, in the colloquy I must think and pray as is appropriate. For example, I may be tempted or consoled; I may want to have one virtue or another; I may want to offer one part of myself or another; I may want to feel sorrow or joy about what I am contemplating. Finally I should ask for that which will most effectively obtain certain particular things I desire.

Thus I can make just one colloquy with Christ our Lord, or if the matter or my devotion moves me, I can make three colloquies, one to the Mother, one to the Son and the other to the Father, as directed in the second week in the meditation on the two standards, with the note that follows the classes of people.

[200] SECOND CONTEMPLATION
In the morning. From the Last Supper up to and including the agony in the garden.

Prayer. The usual preparatory prayer

[201] *First prelude.* The first prelude is the theme. Here it is how Christ our Lord with his eleven disciples came down from Mount Sion, after the Last Supper, into the valley of Joshaphat. He left eight of them in one part of the valley and the other three in the garden. He

began to pray and sweated drops of blood. After that he prayed three times to the Father, and woke his three disciples. Then his enemies fell down at the sound of his voice and Judas kissed him. Peter cut off Malchus' ear and Christ healed it. He was arrested like a criminal and they took him down the valley and then up the hill to the house of Annas.

[202] *Second prelude*. The second prelude is to imagine the place. Here it is to picture the road from Mount Sion to the valley of Josaphat. Likewise the garden, its breadth, its length, its appearance.

[203] *Third prelude*. The third prelude is to ask for what I desire. In the passion it is proper to ask for sorrow with the sorrowing Christ, anguish with Christ in anguish, tears and grief for all the suffering Christ endured for me.

[204] *First note*. After the preparatory prayer and the three preludes above, this second contemplation shall follow the same procedure in the points and the colloquy as in the first contemplation on the Last Supper. At the hour of Mass and Vespers there should be two repetitions of the first and second contemplations, and then after supper apply the senses to the two contemplations, always making the preparatory prayer and the three preludes. This should be adapted to the subject, in the same way as has been explained in the second week.

[205] *Second note*. Depending on age, disposition and health, the retreatant will do five exercises or fewer every day.

[206] *Third note*. In this third week the second and sixth additional directions are to be partly changed. The second will be that when I wake up I am to think about where I am going and for what purpose. I should review the contemplation I am about to make, according to what the subject is, forcing myself while I get up and dress, to grieve and sorrow for all the sorrow and pain suffered by Christ our Lord.

The change in the sixth additional direction will be not to seek joyful thoughts, even though they may be good and holy. For example, rather than thinking about the resurrection and glory I should make myself feel sorrow, pain and heartbreak, by frequently remembering the hardship, sufferings and sorrows of Christ our Lord, from his birth until the mystery of the passion which I am contemplating now.

[207] *Fourth note.* The particular examination of conscience on the present exercises and additional directions shall be made as it was made in the previous week.

[208] *Second day.* At midnight the contemplation will be on the events from the garden to the house of Annas inclusive [291]. In the morning, from Annas' house to the house of Caiaphas inclusive, [292]. There will be two repetitions and the application of the senses as before.

Third day. At midnight, from Caiaphas' house to Pilate inclusive [293]. In the morning, from Pilate to Herod, inclusive [294]. After that the two repetitions and application of the senses as before.

Fourth day. At midnight, from Herod to Pilate [295], using for this contemplation only the first half of what occurred in the house of Pilate. In the morning exercise, the remaining incidents in the same house. Then the repetitions and application of the senses as before.

Fifth day. At midnight, from Pilate's house till Christ is nailed to the cross [296]. In the morning, from his being lifted up on the cross until he dies [297]. Afterwards the two repetitions and application of the senses.

Sixth day. At midnight, from Christ being taken down from the cross to being placed in the tomb exclusive [298]. In the morning from Christ in the tomb up to the house to which Our Lady went after the burial of her Son.

Seventh day. Contemplation of the whole passion in one exercise at midnight, and again in the morning. Instead of the two repetitions and the application of the senses, consider during this whole day as often as possible how Christ our Lord's most sacred body was separated and detached from his soul, and where and how it was buried. Likewise consider the loneliness of Our Lady, with all her sorrow and distress, and that of the disciples.

[209] *Note.* Anyone who wishes to spend more time on the passion must take fewer mysteries in each contemplation. That is, in the first contemplation take only the supper; in the second the washing of feet; in the third the giving of the sacrament; in the fourth Christ's address after the supper and so on for the other contemplations and mysteries.

Likewise after going through the passion, take one day to contemplate the first half of the passion, and a second day for the other half, and a third day for contemplating the passion as a whole.

On the other hand, anyone who wants to spend less time on the passion could choose the supper at midnight; the garden in the morning; Annas' house at the hour of Mass; Caiaphas' house at the hour of Vespers; Pilate's house in the hour before supper. Without doing the repetitions or application of the senses do five different exercises every day, and in each exercise take a different mystery of Christ our Lord. And when you have gone through the whole passion in this way, you can spend another day on the passion on its entirety in one exercise or in various exercises, as seems most helpful.

[210] RULES FOR EATING

First rule. There is less need to abstain from bread because it is not usually a food for which the appetite becomes uncontrollable or temptation so persistent as with other kinds of food.

[211] *Second rule.* The second rule is about drink. Here abstinence seems more necessary than in the case of eating bread. So we should carefully consider what is good for us and allow it, and what is bad for us and reject it.

[212] *Third rule.* The third rule is about food. Partial or complete abstinence is in order here, because the appetite can easily become excessive and develop cravings. So abstinence from food is observed in two ways. Firstly, become accustomed to eating plain food, and secondly, if you eat delicacies, do so sparingly.

[213] *Fourth rule.* Provided care is taken not to fall ill, the more you abstain from what is necessary, the more quickly you will attain the right balance in your eating and drinking, for two reasons. Firstly, by helping yourself and preparing yourself in this way, you will often derive more insights, consolations and divine inspirations to show you what is appropriate. Secondly, if you see that such abstinence does not leave you with enough strength or will for the spiritual exercises you will easily be able to judge how much more food you need to sustain your body.

[214] *Fifth rule.* While you are eating, imagine that you are seeing Christ our Lord eating with his apostles, drinking, looking and speaking. And try to imitate him. Do this in such a way that most of your mind is occupied in considering Our Lord and the lesser part in feeding your body. This will enable you to adopt a better way of governing how you behave and control yourself.

[215] *Sixth rule.* The sixth rule is that while you are eating you can consider other things, such as the life of the saints or some pious thought or some spiritual work you need to do. By attending to such matters you will have less delight and enjoyment in the nourishment of your body.

[216] *Seventh rule.* Above all, you should be careful that your whole mind is not intent upon what you are eating. You should not be so carried away by your appetite that you rush your food. But you should master yourself both in the way you eat as well as in the quantity you eat.

[217] *Eighth rule.* The eighth rule is that in order to overcome the desire for overeating it is very helpful after lunch or supper, or at another time when you have little appetite to eat, to make up your mind about the lunch or supper to come. And thus each day decide on the quantity it is right to eat. You must not give in to your appetite or to temptation. In order to overcome any excessive appetite or temptation by the enemy, if you are tempted to eat more, eat less.

Fourth Week

[218] FIRST CONTEMPLATION
How Christ our Lord appeared to Our Lady [299].

Prayer. The usual preparatory prayer.

[219] *First prelude.* The first prelude is the subject. Here it is how, after Christ died on the cross, his body was separated from his soul but still united to the divinity. His blessed soul, likewise united with the divinity, descended into hell. He released the souls of the just, went to the tomb, rose again and appeared in body and soul to his blessed Mother.

[220] *Second prelude.* The second prelude is to imagine the place. Here it is to see the arrangement of the holy tomb, and then Our Lady's house, looking at its different parts, such as her bedroom, prayer room etc.

[221] *Third prelude.* The third is to ask for what I desire. Here it will be to ask for the grace to be intensely happy and glad at Christ our Lord's glory and joy.

[222] *The first, second and third points.* These will be the same as those for the contemplation on the Lord's supper [190].

[223] *Fourth point.* Consider how the divinity, which appeared to be hidden in the passion, now appears and reveals itself so miraculously in the most holy resurrection, through its true and most sacred effects.

[224] *Fifth point.* The fifth is to look at the comforting done by Christ our Lord and compare it with how friends comfort one another.

[225] *Colloquy*. Close with one or more colloquies, according to the subject matter, and say an *Our Father*.

[226] *First note*. In the following contemplations proceed in all the resurrection mysteries in the manner set out below, up to the ascension. Observe through the whole week of the resurrection the same method that was used for the week of the passion. In this first contemplation of the resurrection adapt the preludes to the subject matter. The five points are the same and so are the additional directions set out below. And in everything else follow the pattern of the passion week, in the repetitions, application of the five senses, lengthening or shortening of the mystery etc.

[227] *Second note*. Generally, in this fourth week it is more suitable than in the preceding three weeks to do four exercises instead of five. Do the first on getting up in the morning, the second at the hour of Mass or before lunch, instead of the first repetition; the third at the hour of Vespers instead of the second repetition; the fourth before supper, applying the five senses to the three exercises of that day, noting and pausing at the principal parts and where you have felt more emotion or spiritual delight.

[228] *Third note*. Although in all the contemplations a fixed number of points is given, three or five etc., the person contemplating can take more or fewer points according to what is found better. It is very helpful before beginning the contemplation to look ahead and work out the number of points to be taken.

[229] *Fourth note*. In this fourth week the second, sixth, seventh and tenth additional directions are to be changed.

The second will be, as soon as I awake, set before my mind the contemplation I am to make and try to feel moved and happy at the great joy and happiness of Christ our Lord.

The sixth is to call to mind and think about things that cause pleasure, happiness and spiritual joy, such as the glory of heaven.

The seventh is to make use of light and pleasant weather, such as freshness in summer or sun and warmth in winter, as much as the soul feels these can help it to rejoice in its Creator and Redeemer.

The tenth, instead of penance, to concentrate on temperance and moderation in everything, unless it is the time when fasting or abstinence is prescribed by the Church, because these must always be observed unless there is a genuine reason for not doing so.

[230] CONTEMPLATION TO ATTAIN THE LOVE OF GOD

Note. It is appropriate to note two things. The first is that love should show itself in deeds more than in words.

[231] The second is that love consists of mutual communication. So the lover gives and communicates to the beloved what he has or from what he has and can do, and vice versa, the beloved does likewise to the lover. So if one has knowledge, he should give this to the one who has not. The same goes for honours, wealth and so on.

Prayer. The usual preparatory prayer.

[232] *First prelude*. The first prelude is to imagine the place. Here it is to see how I stand before God our Lord, the angels and saints interceding for me.

[233] *Second prelude*. The second prelude is to ask for what I desire. Here it will be to ask for inner knowledge of all the good I have received, so that I can recognise it wholly and love and serve God in all things.

[234] *First point*. The first point is to call to mind the blessings of creation and redemption, and the special favours I have received. With great affection I ponder how much God our Lord has done for me and how much he has given me of what he has. Consequently I recall how this same Lord wants to give himself to me as far as his divine nature allows. Then I reflect on myself, considering what is reasonable and right for me to offer to the Divine Majesty. All my possessions and myself with them I offer with great affection:

> *Take, Lord, and receive all my freedom, my memory, my understanding and my will, all I have and possess. You have given all to me, to you, Lord, I return it. All is yours, dispose it wholly according to your will. Give me your love and grace, for that is sufficient for me.*

[235] *Second point*. The second point is to reflect how God dwells in creatures, in the elements, giving them being; in plants, giving them growth; in animals, giving them sensation; and in human beings, giving them understanding. Thus he dwells in me giving me being, life, sensation and understanding. Likewise I reflect on how I have

become a temple by being created in the image and likeness of God. I also reflect on myself, in the way set out in the first point and in any other way I feel may help. I will do the same for each point that follows.

[236] *Third point.* The third point is to consider how God works and toils for me in all created things on the face of the earth. He works in the heavens, elements, fruits, cattle etc., giving being, keeping them in being, giving growth, sensation etc. Then I reflect on myself.

[237] *Fourth point.* The fourth point is to consider how all blessings and gifts come down from above. For example, my limited power descends from the supreme and infinite power above. Likewise justice, goodness, pity, mercy etc., just as rays come down from the sun, and rivers from springs etc. Then I will reflect on myself, as already mentioned, and conclude with a colloquy and an *Our Father*.

[238] THREE METHODS OF PRAYER.
THE TEN COMMANDMENTS

The first method of prayer is on the ten commandments, the seven deadly sins, the three powers of the soul, and the five senses. This method of prayer is not meant so much to give a form and method of prayer properly so called, but rather to supply a way of proceeding and some exercises by which the soul may prepare itself and make progress so that its prayer may be acceptable to God.

[239] First, do something equivalent to the second additional direction of the second week. That is, before beginning to pray, rest your spirit a little by sitting down or walking, as seems best. Consider where I am going and for what purpose. This same addition is to be done at the beginning of all methods of prayer.

[240] Prepara*tory prayer.* I ask for grace from God our Lord, so that I may know how I have failed to keep the ten commandments, and likewise to ask for grace and help to do better in future. I ask for perfect understanding of them to keep them better and for the greater glory and praise of the Divine Majesty.

[241] In this first method of prayer I begin by considering and thinking over the first commandment. I reflect on how I have kept it and

how I have broken it. I generally keep considering this for the time it takes to say three Our Fathers and three *Hail Marys*. If during this time I discover my faults I ask pardon for them and say an *Our Father*. Do the same with each of the ten commandments.

[242] *First note.* When you come to consider a commandment in which you find you have no habit of sinning, it is not necessary to spend so much time on it. The more often you have broken a commandment the more time you should spend on considering and examining it, and if less often, then less time spent is adequate. The same applies for the deadly sins.

[243] *Second note.* After having gone through all the commandments in this way, accusing myself when I have broken them and asking for grace and help to do better in future, I will finish with a colloquy with God our Lord, on the same subject.

[244] THE DEADLY SINS

As far as the seven deadly sins are concerned, follow the additional direction and the preparatory prayer in the way described. The only difference is that here we are concerned with sins that must be avoided, whereas before it was commandments to be kept. Otherwise keep to the same order and method and the colloquy.

[245] In order to become more aware of the faults you have committed relating to the seven deadly sins, consider their opposites. And to avoid these sins, resolve and endeavour through devout exercises to acquire and practise the seven opposite virtues.

[246] THE POWERS OF THE SOUL

With regard to the powers of the soul, keep to the same order and method as in the commandments, following the additional direction, preparatory prayer and colloquy.

[247] THE FIVE BODILY SENSES

With regard to the five bodily senses, still keep the same order, changing the subject matter as required.

[248] *Note.* If you want to imitate Christ our Lord in the use of his senses, commend yourself to him in the preparatory prayer. After considering each sense say a *Hail Mary* or an *Our Father*. If you want to imitate Our Lady in the use of the senses, commend yourself to her in the preparatory prayer, asking to obtain the grace for you to do so from her Son and Lord. After considering each of the senses, say a *Hail Mary*.

[249] THE SECOND METHOD OF PRAYER

The second method of prayer consists in carefully considering the meaning of each word in the prayer.

[250] *Additional direction.* The same as in the first method of prayer [239].

[251] *Preparatory prayer.* The preparatory prayer should be made to suit the person to whom it is addressed.

[252] The second method of prayer is to kneel or stand, according to which position you find most conducive to devotion, close your eyes or fix them on one spot without letting them wander. Say *Our Father* and keep meditating on it for as long as you find meaning, comparisons, delight, and consolation in the consideration of it. Then do the same for each word of the *Our Father* or any other prayer you wish to pray in this way.

[253] *First rule.* The first rule is to spend a whole hour in this manner on the *Our Father*. When you have finished say a *Hail Mary*, the *Creed*, the *Anima Christi* and *Hail Holy Queen* vocally or mentally, in the usual way.

[254] *Second rule.* The second rule is that if while you are meditating on the *Our Father* you find in one or two words such good food for thought and delight and consolation, then do not be anxious to go on any further, even though you may spend the whole hour on what you have found. When time has run out, say the rest of the *Our Father* in the usual way.

[255] *Third rule.* The third rule is that if you spent a whole hour on one or two words of the *Our Father,* when you return to the prayer on another day, say the word or words in the usual way and then immediately begin contemplating on the next word, according to what was said in the second rule.

[256] *First note.* When the *Our Father* is finished in one day or many, then do the same with the *Hail Mary* and then with the other prayers, so that for a certain period you are continually exercising in one of them.

[257] *Second note.* When you have finished praying, turn to the person you have been praying to and ask in a few words for the virtues or graces you feel yourself to be most in need of.

[258] THE THIRD METHOD OF PRAYER
The third method of prayer is a measured rhythmical recitation.

Additional direction. Same as for the first and second methods.

Preparatory prayer. The preparatory prayer will be as in the second method of prayer.

The third method of prayer is as follows. Each breath is timed to coincide with a prayer, so that one word of the *Our Father* or another prayer being prayed takes the space of one breath. From one breath to the next you concentrate on the meaning of this word, or on the person you are praying to, or on your own unworthiness, or on the difference between such loftiness and such unworthiness. Do the same for the other words of the *Our Father.* The other prayers, that is, the *Hail Mary, Anima Christi,* the *Creed,* the *Hail Holy Queen* are to be said in the usual way.

[259] *First rule.* The first rule is that on another day or at another hour when you wish to pray, say the *Hail Mary* in this measured rhythmical way, and the other prayers in the ordinary way.

[260] *Second rule.* The second rule is that if you want to spend longer with this method of prayer, you can say all the above prayers or part of them in this way, as explained.

[261] THE MYSTERIES OF THE LIFE OF CHRIST OUR LORD

Note. For each mystery three points will usually be given to make it easier to meditate and contemplate on them.

[262] The annunciation to Our Lady. *See Luke 1:26-38*

First point. The angel Gabriel greeted Our Lady and told her about the conception of Christ our Lord: And the angel came to Mary and said, 'Hail, full of grace... you will conceive in your womb and bear a son.'

Second point. The angel confirms what he has told Our Lady by announcing the conception of St John the Baptist, saying:

'Behold your kinswoman Elizabeth in her old age has also conceived a son.'

Third point. Our Lady replies to the angel: 'Behold the handmaid of the Lord; let it be to me according to your word.'

[263] The visitation of Our Lady to St Elizabeth. *See Luke 1:39-56.*

First point. When Our Lady visited St Elizabeth, St John the Baptist who was in his mother's womb, felt the presence of Our Lady. And when Elizabeth heard the greeting of Mary, the babe leaped in her womb; and Elizabeth was filled with the Holy Spirit and exclaimed with a loud cry, 'Blessed are you among women, and blessed is the fruit of your womb.'

Second point. Our Lady sings the *Magnificat*: My soul glorifies the Lord.

Third point. Mary remained with Elizabeth about three months, and returned to her home.

[264] The birth of Christ our Lord. *See Luke 2:1-14.*

First point. Our Lady and her husband Joseph go from Nazareth to Bethlehem. And Joseph went up from Galilee, from the city of Nazareth... to Bethlehem... to be enrolled with Mary, his betrothed, who was with child.

Second point. She gave birth to her first-born son and wrapped him in swaddling cloths and laid him in a manger.

Third point. And suddenly there was with the angel a multitude of the heavenly host praising God and saying, 'Glory to God in the highest.'

[265] The shepherds. *See Luke 2:8-20.*

First point. The birth of Christ our Lord is revealed to the shepherds by the angel. 'I bring you good news of great joy... for to you is born this day... a Saviour.'

Second point. The shepherds go to Bethlehem. And they went with haste, and found Mary and Joseph and the babe lying in a manger.

Third point. The shepherds returned, glorifying and praising God.

[266] The circumcision. *See Luke 2:21*

First point. They circumcised the Child Jesus.

Second point. He was called Jesus, the name given by the angel before he was conceived in the womb.

Third point. They returned the child to his Mother, who felt tenderly towards her Son because of the blood he would shed.

[267] The three wise men. *See Matthew 2:1-12*

First point. The three wise men, guided by a star, came to worship Jesus saying: We have seen his star in the east and have come to worship him.

Second point. They worshipped him and offered him gifts: They fell down and worshipped him. Then opening their treasures, they offered him gifts, gold and frankincense and myrrh.

Third point. Being warned in a dream not to return to Herod, they departed to their own country by another way.

[268] The purification of Our Lady and the presentation of the child Jesus. *See Luke 2:22-39.*

First point. They bring the Child Jesus to the temple, to be presented to the Lord as the first-born and they offer for him a pair of turtle doves or two young pigeons.

Second point. Coming into the temple Simeon took him in his arms... and said, 'Lord, now let your servant depart in peace.'

Third point. Anna coming up at that very hour gave thanks to God, and spoke of him to all who were looking for the redemption of Israel.

[269] The flight into Egypt. *See Matthew 2:13-18.*

First point. Herod wanted to kill the child Jesus and so he killed the innocents. Before their death the angel warned Joseph to flee into Egypt: 'Rise, take the child and his mother and flee to Egypt.'

Second point. They left for Egypt. He rose and took the child and his mother by night and departed to Egypt.

Third point. He remained there until the death of Herod.

[270] How our Lord returned from Egypt. *See Matthew 2:19-23.*

First point. The angel tells Joseph to return to Israel: 'Rise, take the child and his mother, and go to the land of Israel.'

Second point. He rose and took the child and his mother and went to the land of Israel.

Third point. But when he heard that Archelaus, Herod's son, was king in Judaea, he retired to Nazareth.

[271] Christ our Lord's life from the age of twelve to thirty. *See Luke 2:51-52.*

First point. He was obedient to his parents.

Second point. Jesus increased in wisdom and in stature, and in favour with God and man.

Third point. He seems to have practised the craft of carpentry, as St Mark indicates in chapter six: 'Is not this the carpenter?'

[272] Christ's coming to the temple when he was twelve years old. *See Luke 2:41-50.*

First point. At the age of twelve Christ our Lord went up from Nazareth to Jerusalem.

Second point. Christ our Lord remained in Jerusalem and his parents did not know.

Third point. After three days they found him disputing in the temple, sitting among the doctors. When his parents asked him where he had been, he answered: 'Did you not know that I must be about my Father's business?'

[273] The baptism of Christ. *See Matthew 3:13-17.*

First point. After taking leave of his blessed mother, Christ our Lord came from Nazareth to the River Jordan, where St John the Baptist was.

Second point. St John baptised Christ our Lord. He tried to excuse himself, saying he was unworthy to baptise him. Christ said to John: 'Let it be so now; for thus it is fitting for us to fulfil all righteousness.'

Third point. The Holy Spirit descended on him in bodily form, as a dove, and a voice came from heaven: 'You are my beloved Son; with you I am well pleased.'

[274] The temptation of Christ. *See Luke 4:1-13 and Matthew 4:1-11.*

First point. After he was baptised he went to the wilderness, where he fasted for forty days and forty nights.

Second point. He was tempted three times by the enemy: 'If you are the Son of God command these stones to become loaves of bread...Throw yourself down... All these I will give you if you will fall down and worship me.'

Third point. The angels came and ministered to him.

[275] The calling of the apostles

First point. It appears that St Peter and St Andrew were called three times: first to some understanding of Christ, as we read in the first chapter of St John. Secondly, to follow Christ in a way, with the intention of returning to the possessions they had left, as we read in St Luke chapter five. Thirdly, to follow Christ our Lord for ever, as we read in St Matthew chapter four and St Mark chapter one.

Second point. He called Philip, as we find in the first chapter of St John, and Matthew, as Matthew himself relates in his ninth chapter.

Third point. He called the other apostles but the Gospel does not give an account of their particular calling.

We should also consider three things: firstly, that the apostles belonged to an uneducated low social class. Secondly, the dignity of the office to which they were so graciously called. Thirdly, the gifts and graces by which they were raised above all the Fathers of the Old and New Testaments.

[276] The first miracle at the marriage feast at Cana in Galilee. *See John 2:1-11.*

First point. Christ our Lord and his disciples were invited to the wedding.

Second point. The Mother tells her Son they have run out of wine saying: 'They have no wine.' And she told the servants: 'Do whatever he tells you.'

Third point. He changed the water into wine and manifested his glory and his disciples believed in him.

[277] How Christ our Lord drove the sellers out of the temple. *See John 2:13-22.*

First point. He drove all the sellers out of the temple with a whip made of cords.

Second point. He upset the tables and the money belonging to the rich bankers who were in the temple.

Third point. He gently told the poor who were selling doves: 'Take these things away; you shall not make my Father's house a house of trade.'

[278] The Sermon on the Mount. *See Matthew chapter 5.*

First point. He speaks to his beloved disciples apart on the eight beatitudes. Blessed are the poor in spirit..., the meek..., the merciful..., those who mourn..., those who hunger and thirst for justice..., the peacemakers..., those who are persecuted...

Second point. He exhorts them to make good use of their talents. Let your light so shine before men, that they may see your good works and give glory to your Father who is in heaven.

Third point. He shows that he does not break the law but fulfils it. He declares the precepts of not killing, not committing adultery, not swearing falsely and loving our enemies. I say to you, love your enemies and do good to those who hate you.

[279] Christ calms the storm. *See Matthew 8:23-27.*

First point. While Christ our Lord was sleeping in the boat, a great storm arose on the lake.

Second point. His disciples were terrified and woke him up. He reproached them for their lack of faith saying: 'Why are you afraid, o men of little faith?'

Third point. He commanded the wind and the sea to stop. The sea became calm and the disciples were amazed saying: 'What sort of a man is this that even winds and sea obey him?'

[280] How Christ walked on the water. *See Matthew 14:22-33.*

First point. Christ remained on the mountain and told his disciples to get into the boat. He dismissed the crowds and remained alone to pray.

Second point. The boat was tossed by the waves and Christ came to it walking on the water. The disciples thought he was a ghost.

Third point. Christ said to them: 'It is I. Do not be afraid.'

At his command St Peter went to him walking on the water, but he doubted and began to sink. Christ our Lord rescued him and rebuked him for his little faith. Later, when he boarded the boat, the wind dropped.

[281] How the apostles were sent out to preach. *See Matthew 10:1-16.*

First point. Christ calls his beloved disciples and gives them power to cast out demons from human bodies and to cure all diseases.

Second point. He teaches them prudence and patience: 'I send you out as sheep in the midst of wolves; so be wise as serpents and innocent as doves.'

Third point. He tells them how to go: 'Take no gold, nor silver... you have received freely, so give freely.' And he tells them what to say: 'And preach as you go, saying: 'The kingdom of heaven is at hand.'

[282] The conversion of Mary Magdalene. *See Luke 7:36-50.*

First point. Mary comes into the Pharisee's house where Christ our Lord is sitting at table. She brings an alabaster jar of ointment.

Second point. At Our Lord's feet, she begins to wash them with her tears and wipes them with the hair, and kisses his feet and anoints them with ointment.

Third point. When the Pharisee accuses Mary Magdalene, Christ defends her, saying: 'Therefore, I tell you, her sins, which are many are forgiven, for she loved much... and he said to the woman, Your sins are forgiven... Your faith has saved you; go in peace.'

[283] How Christ our Lord fed the five thousand. *See Matthew 14:13-21.*

First point. As it was getting late, the disciples asked Christ to dismiss the crowd who were with him.

Second point. Christ our Lord ordered them to bring loaves of bread and make the crowd to sit down. He blessed, broke and gave the loaves to his disciples. And the disciples gave them to the crowd.

Third point. And they all ate and were satisfied. And they took up twelve baskets full of the broken pieces left over.

[284] The transfiguration of Christ. *See Matthew 17:1-9.*

First point. Taking with him his three beloved disciples, Peter, James and John, Christ was transfigured, and his face shone like the sun, and his clothes became white as snow.

Second point. He spoke with Moses and Elijah.

Third point. St Peter said they should make three tents and a voice came from heaven saying: 'This is my beloved Son, with whom I am well pleased; listen to him.' When his disciples heard the voice, they were so afraid they fell on their faces. Christ our Lord touched them and said: 'Rise and have no fear... Tell no one the vision until the Son of man is raised from the dead.'

[285] The raising of Lazarus. *See John 11:1-45.*

First point. Martha and Mary let Christ our Lord know Lazarus is ill. He purposely stays on for two more days so that the miracle may be more obvious.

Second point. Before he raises Lazarus he asks both the women to believe, saying: 'I am the resurrection and the life; he who believes in me, though he may die, yet shall he live.'

Third point. Jesus wept. Then he prayed and then he raised Lazarus. The way he raised him from the dead was by commanding: 'Lazarus, come out!'

[286] The supper at Bethany. *See Matthew 26:6-10.*

First point. The Lord has supper in Simon the leper's house, together with Lazarus.

Second point. Mary pours the ointment on Christ's head.

Third point. Judas grumbles, saying: 'Why this waste?' Jesus excuses Mary Magdalene again saying: 'Why do you trouble the woman. For she has done a beautiful thing to me.'

[287] Palm Sunday. *See Matthew 21:1-17.*

First point. Our Lord sends for the donkey and the colt saying: 'Untie them and bring them to me. If anyone says anything to you, you shall say, "The Lord needs them," and he will send them immediately.

Second point. He mounts the donkey covered with the apostles' cloaks.

Third point. They come out to meet him, laying their cloaks on the road and branches from the trees. They cry: 'Hosanna to the Son of David! Blessed be he who comes in the name of the Lord! Hosanna in the highest!'

[288] The preaching in the temple. *See Luke 19:47-8.*

First point. He was preaching every day in the temple.

Second point. When he had finished preaching, because he had no one to lodge with in Jerusalem he returned to Bethany.

[289] The Last Supper. *See Matthew 26:20-30; John 13:1-30.*

First point. He ate the paschal lamb with his twelve apostles and predicted his death to them: 'Truly, I say to you, one of you will betray me.'

Second point. He washed his disciples' feet, even Judas'. He began with St Peter, who was unwilling in view of the Lord's majesty and his own unworthiness: 'Lord, do you wash my feet?' But St Peter did not realise that in doing this Jesus was giving an example of humility: 'I have given you an example, that you also should do as I have done to you.'

Third point. He instituted the most holy sacrifice of the Eucharist, as a very great sign of his love, saying: 'Take and eat.' After supper Judas went out to sell Christ our Lord.

[290] From the Last Supper to the agony in the garden. *See Matthew 26:30-46; Mark 14:26-42; Luke 22:39-46; John 18:1-11.*

First point. After finishing supper and singing the hymn, the Lord went out to the Mount of Olives, with his disciples who were full of fear. Leaving eight of them in Gethsemane, he said: 'Sit here, while I go yonder and pray.'

Second point. Accompanied by Sts Peter, James and John, he prayed three times to the Lord, saying: 'My Father, if it be possible, let this cup pass from me; nevertheless, not as I will, but as you will.' And being in an agony he prayed more earnestly.

[291] From the Garden to the house of Annas. *See Matthew 26:47-58; Mark 14:43-68; Luke 22:47-57; John 18:12-24.*

First point. First the Lord allows Judas to kiss him and lets himself be arrested like a thief. He says to them: 'Have you come out as against a robber, with swords and clubs? When I was with you day after day in the temple, you did not lay hands on me.' When he said, 'Who are you looking for?' his enemies fell to the ground.

Second point. St Peter wounds a servant of the high priest. Our Lord says to him: 'Put your sword back in its place.' And he heals the servant's wound.

Third point. Abandoned by his disciples he is taken to Annas, where St Peter, who has followed him from a distance, denies him once. Christ is hit as they say: 'Is that how you answer the high priest?'

[292] From the house of Annas to the house of Caiaphas. *See Matthew 26; Mark 14; Luke 22; John 18.*

First point. They take him tied up from Annas' house to the house of Caiaphas. Here St Peter denies him thrice. The Lord looks at him and he went out and wept bitterly.

Second point. Jesus remained tied up for the whole night.

Third point. Those who kept him prisoner mocked him, wounded him, blindfolded him and punched him. They said to him: 'Prophesy! Who is it that struck you?' And they spoke many other words against him, reviling him.

[293] From Caiaphas' house to Pilate's house. *See Matthew 27; Mark 15; Luke 23; John 18.*

First point. The Jews took Jesus to Pilate. They accused him before Pilate saying: 'We found this man perverting our nation, and forbidding us to give tribute to Caesar.'

Second point. After Pilate had examined him several times he said: 'I find no crime in this man.'

Third point. The people preferred Barabbas the thief to him. But they all cried out together, 'Away with this man and release to us Barabbas.'

[294] From Pilate's house to Herod's. *See Luke 23:6-11.*

First point. Pilate sent the Galilean Jesus to Herod, who was tetrarch of Galilee.

Second point. Herod was curious and questioned him at length. Jesus did not answer anything, even though the scribes and priests kept accusing him.

Third point. Herod and his court mocked Jesus and clothed him in a white robe.

[295] From Herod's house to Pilate's . *See Matthew 27; Mark 15; Luke 23; John 19.*

First point. Herod sent him back to Pilate. In this way they became friends, having been enemies before.

Second point. Pilate took Jesus and flogged him and the soldiers made a crown of thorns and put it on his head. They dressed him in a purple robe, came before him and said: 'Hail, King of the Jews!' And they struck him.

Third point. Pilate brought him out for all to see. So Jesus came out, wearing the crown of thorns and the purple robe. Pilate said to them, 'Here is the man!' When the chief priests and the officers saw him, they cried out, 'Crucify him, crucify him!'

[296] From Pilate's house to the Cross

First point. Pilate sitting on the judgement seat gave Jesus to them to crucify, after the Jews had denied he was their king saying: 'We have no king but Caesar.'

Second point. He carried the cross on his shoulders, and when he could no longer carry it, Simon of Cyrene was compelled to carry it after him.

Third point. They crucified him between two thieves, placing this title above him: Jesus of Nazareth, the King of the Jews.

[297] Jesus dies on the Cross. *See John 19:23-37.*

First point. He spoke seven words on the cross: he prayed for those who were crucifying him; he forgave the thief; he entrusted St John to his Mother and his Mother to St John; he said with a loud voice, 'I am thirsty'; and they gave him gall mixed with vinegar; he said, 'he was forsaken'; he said, 'It is done.' He said, 'Father into your hands I commend my spirit.'

Second point. The sun was darkened, the rocks split; the graves opened, the veil of the temple was torn in two from top to bottom.

Third point. They blasphemed against him saying: 'Aha! You who would destroy the temple and build it in three days, save yourself, and come down from the cross!' They divided his clothes among them. When his side was pierced with a lance, blood and water flowed from it.

[298] From the cross to the sepulchre. *See John 19:23-37.*

First point. He was taken down from the cross by Joseph and Nicodemus, in the presence of his sorrowing Mother.

Second point. His body was laid in the tomb, anointed and buried.

Third point. Guards were stationed.

[299] The resurrection of Christ our Lord and his first appearance

First point. He appeared first to the Virgin Mary. Although this is not mentioned in scripture, still it is considered as mentioned when he says he appeared to so many others. For the scripture expects us to have understanding, since it is written: 'Are you also without understanding?'

[300] Second appearance. *See Mark 26:1-11.*

First point. Very early in the morning Mary Magdalene, Mary the mother of James, and Salome go to the tomb saying: 'Who will roll away the stone for us from the door of the tomb?'

Second point. They saw the stone had been rolled away and an angel, who said: 'Do not be amazed; you seek Jesus of Nazareth, who was crucified. He has risen, he is not here.'

Third point. He appeared to Mary Magdalene, who remained at the tomb after the other women had gone.

[301] Third appearance. *See Matthew, last chapter.*

First point. The two Marys left the tomb with fear and great joy, wanting to announce to the disciples the resurrection of the Lord.

Second point. Christ our Lord appeared to them on the way, saying, 'Greetings.'

Third point. Jesus says to them: 'Do not be afraid; go and tell my brothers to go to Galilee; there they will see me.'

[302] Fourth appearance. *See Luke 24:9-12; 33-44.*

First point. When he heard from the women that Christ had risen, St Peter hurried to the tomb.

Second point. Entering the tomb he saw only the cloths with which Christ our Lord's body had been covered and nothing else.

Third point. While he was thinking about these things, Christ appeared to him and so the apostles said: 'The Lord has risen indeed, and has appeared to Simon!'

[303] Fifth appearance. *See Luke, last chapter.*

First point. He appears to the disciples who were going to Emmaus and were talking about Christ.

Second point. He rebukes them, proving from scripture that Christ had to die and rise again: 'O foolish men, and slow of heart to believe all that the prophets have spoken! Was it not necessary that the Christ should suffer these things and enter into his glory?'

Third point. At their request he stayed there and remained with them until he gave them communion and disappeared. On their return they told the disciples how they had recognised him in the communion.

[304] Sixth appearance. *See John 20:19-23.*

First point. All the disciples were gathered together 'for fear of the Jews', except St Thomas.

Second point. Jesus appeared to them, even though the doors were shut, and standing amongst them he said: 'Peace be with you!'

Third point. He gave them the Holy Spirit, saying to them: 'Receive the Holy Spirit. If you forgive the sins of any, they are forgiven.'

[305] Seventh appearance. *See John 20:24-29.*

First point. St Thomas did not believe because he had not been present at the previous appearance. He said: 'Unless I see in his hands the print of the nails, and place my finger in the mark of the nails, and place my hand in his side, I will not believe.'

Second point. Jesus appeared eight days later, while the doors were shut, and said to St Thomas: 'Put your finger here, and see my hands, and put out your hand, and place it in my side; do not be faithless, but believing.'

Third point. St Thomas believed and said: 'My Lord and my God!' Christ answered: 'Blessed are those who have not seen and yet believed.'

[306] Eighth appearance. *See John, last chapter.*

First point. Jesus appeared to seven of his disciples who were fishing. All night long they had caught nothing. They cast their net again when Jesus told them to and they were not able to haul it in, for the quantity of fish.

Second point. Through this miracle St John recognised him and said to St Peter: 'It is the Lord!' Whereupon Peter jumped into the sea to come to Jesus.

Third point. He gave them some grilled fish to eat and a honeycomb. He entrusted the sheep to St Peter, first asking him three times if he loved him. Then he said: 'Feed my sheep.'

[307] Ninth appearance. *See Matthew 28:16-20.*

First point. At the Lord's order the disciples go to Mount Tabor.

Second point. Christ appears to them and says: 'All authority in heaven and on earth has been given to me.'

Third point. He sends them to preach throughout the world, saying: 'Go and make disciples of all nations, baptising them in the name of the Father and of the Son and of the Holy Spirit.'

[308] Tenth appearance. *See 1 Corinthians 15:6.*

Then he appeared to more than five hundred brothers and sisters at one time.

[309] Eleventh appearance. *See 1 Corinthians 15:7.*

Then he appeared to James.

[310] Twelfth appearance

He appeared to Joseph of Arimathea, according to the Lives of the Saints.

[311] Thirteenth appearance. *See 1 Corinthians 15:8.*

He appeared after his ascension to St Paul, 'Last of all, as to one untimely born, he appeared also to me'.

He also appeared in soul to the holy fathers in limbo. After he had got them out and had resumed his body, he often appeared to the disciples and conversed with them.

[312] The ascension of Christ our Lord . *See Acts 1:1-12.*

First point. After appearing to the apostles over a period of forty days, giving many proofs and signs and speaking with them about the kingdom of God, he sent them to await the promised Holy Spirit in Jerusalem.

Second point. He took them out to the Mount of Olives and as they were looking on he was lifted up and a cloud took him out of their sight.

Third point. While they were gazing into heaven, the angels said to them: 'Men of Galilee, why do you stand looking upto heaven? This Jesus, who was taken up from you into heaven, will come in the same way as you saw him go up into heaven.'

[313] RULES FOR THE DISCERNMENT OF SPIRITS

Rules which give a measure of assistance for perceiving and examining the various stirrings felt in the soul: the good ones to be welcomed and the bad ones to be rejected. These rules are most suitable for the first week.

[314] *First rule.* In the case of those who go from one mortal sin to

another, the enemy generally sets before them apparent pleasures, causing them to imagine sensual pleasures and delights, in order to trap them and plunge them deeper into their vices and sins. In these people the good spirit acts in the opposite way, pricking their consciences with remorse through the judgement of their reason.

[315] *Second rule.* In those who are seriously trying to purify themselves of their sins, and progress in the service of God our Lord, the opposite to what is noted in the first rule occurs. In this case it is the evil spirit who causes anxiety and sadness and places obstacles in the way, disturbing them in order to hinder progress. The good spirit gives courage and strength, consolation, tears, inspiration and peace, making things easy and removing all obstacles, so that the good work may go forward.

[316] *Third rule.* Spiritual consolation. I call it consolation when there is some inner stirring in the soul, which sets it on fire with love for its Creator and Lord. Then it cannot love any creature on the face of the earth for its own sake, but only in the Creator of all of them. Likewise when it cries it is for love of its Lord, either for sorrow at its sins, or for the passion of Christ our Lord, or for other things directly related to his service and praise. Finally, I call consolation any increase of hope, faith and charity and any inner joy which calls and draws the soul to heavenly things and its own salvation, giving it rest and peace in its Creator and Lord.

[317] *Fourth rule.* Spiritual desolation. I call desolation everything that is the opposite of the third rule: such as darkness of the soul, disturbance, attraction towards low and earthly things, anxiety from various agitations and temptations jeopardising its faith, hope and love, making it lazy, lukewarm, and as if cut off from its Creator and Lord. For just as consolation is the opposite of desolation, the thoughts arising from consolation are the opposite of those arising from desolation.

[318] *Fifth rule.* In time of desolation never make a change, but remain firm and constant in the intention and determination you had the day before this desolation. For just as in consolation the good spirit guides and leads us, so in desolation it is the evil spirit who counsels us so that we cannot make correct decisions.

[319] *Sixth rule*. Although in desolation we must never change our previous resolutions, it is very helpful to intensify our efforts to combat the desolation. For example, we can be more earnest in prayer, meditation and in examining ourselves more carefully and increasing the penance we do in an appropriate way.

[320] *Seventh rule*. If you are suffering desolation, consider that the Lord has left you to test your natural powers to resist the various agitations and temptations of the enemy. You can do this with divine help, which always remains, even though you may not feel it clearly, because the Lord has withdrawn his gift of great fervour, ardent love and abundant grace. Nevertheless he leaves you with sufficient grace for eternal salvation.

[321] *Eighth rule*. If you are suffering from desolation, strive to be patient, which is the opposite of the vexations troubling you. Think that you will soon be consoled and do all you can to combat the desolation, as was said in the sixth rule.

[322] *Ninth rule*. There are three main reasons for desolation. The first is because we have been lukewarm, lazy or negligent in our spiritual exercises, and so spiritual consolation is withdrawn from us through our own fault. The second reason is to test us to see how strong we are and how long we can continue to serve and praise God without the reward of consolations and special graces. The third is because God wishes to give us a true knowledge and understanding of ourselves so that we may realise that it is not in our power to attain or possess great devotion, intense love, tears or any other spiritual consolation, but that all this is a gift from God our Lord. This teaches us not to rely on ourselves or be swollen with pride or vanity through attributing to ourselves the devotion or any other spiritual consolation.

[323] *Tenth rule*. If you are receiving consolation, think about what it will be like when desolation comes and store up new strength to deal with it.

[324] *Eleventh rule*. If you are receiving consolation, try to humiliate and abase yourself as much as possible thinking how feeble you will be in time of desolation without this grace or consolation. On the

other hand, if you are suffering desolation, remember that you can do a great deal with sufficient grace to resist all your enemies, drawing strength from our Creator and Lord.

[325] *Twelfth rule*. The enemy behaves like a woman in being weak in physical force but strong in will. When she is quarrelling with a man, it is in a woman's nature to falter and back down if the man stands up to her firmly, but if the man begins to falter and back down, then her rage, spite and ferocity increases and knows no bounds. Likewise, it is the enemy's nature to weaken and falter and withdraw his temptations, when the person exercising in spiritual matters stands up to these temptations firmly. On the other hand, if the retreatant begins to be afraid and loses the courage to confront temptations, there is no fiercer beast on the face of the earth than the enemy of human nature in pursuing his wicked intentions ever more viciously.

[326] *Thirteenth rule*. He also behaves like a lover who is false and wants to keep things secret and undiscovered. For just as a man with dishonourable intentions may try to lure away the daughter of some good father or the wife of a good husband, he wants his words and enticements to be kept secret. The opposite annoys him greatly. If the daughter tells her father or the wife her husband about his false words and dishonourable intentions, he realises he cannot pursue his plan. Likewise, when the enemy of human nature tries his cunning inducements on the just soul, he wants them to be received and kept secret. He is very annoyed if the person reveals them to a good confessor or other spiritual person, who is aware of the enemy's deceit and malice. Then the enemy realises he cannot succeed in his evil intention, because he has been found out.

[327] *Fourteenth rule*. Our enemy also behaves like a conquering commander who takes what he wants. Like a captain or leader of an army, he disposes his troops and inspects the fortifications and disposition of the castle in order to attack it at its weakest point. Likewise, the enemy of human nature roams around and inspects all our theological, cardinal and moral virtues. He attacks us and tries to storm us where he finds our defences are weakest and the least adequate for our eternal salvation.

[328] FURTHER RULES FOR THE DISCERNMENT OF SPIRITS
These rules are more suitable for the second week.

[329] *First rule.* It belongs to God and his angels to give true happiness and spiritual joy, dispelling all sadness and dismay induced by the enemy. The enemy's nature is to combat this joy and spiritual consolation, suggesting apparent reasons, subtleties and falsehoods.

[330] *Second rule.* Only God our Lord can give consolation to the soul without any preceding cause. For it is the prerogative of the Creator to go in and out of the soul, act upon it, drawing it wholly towards love for him. When I say without preceding cause, I mean without any previous feeling or knowledge of some object by which this consolation might come through acts of understanding and will.

[331] *Third rule.* It is possible for the soul to be consoled either by the good angel or by the evil angel, for opposite ends. The good angel consoles the soul for the soul's own benefit, so that it may grow and make progress. On the other hand, the evil angel seeks to draw the soul into his own wicked and malicious trap.

[332] *Fourth rule.* The evil angel can transform himself into an angel of light and then enter the devout soul and have his way. That is, he will induce good and holy thoughts to this just soul, but then little by little he contrives to achieve his end by drawing the soul into his secret wiles and perverse intentions.

[333] *Fifth rule.* We must carefully watch the direction of our thoughts. If the beginning, middle and end are all good, and directed towards the good, it is a sign of the good angel. But if as our thoughts develop they lead to something bad or distracting, or less good than what the soul previously proposed, or if they weaken or distress or dismay the soul and take away the peace, tranquillity and calm it had beforehand, this is a clear signal that it is the work of the evil spirit, the enemy of our progress and eternal salvation.

[334] *Sixth rule.* When the enemy of human nature has been perceived and recognised by the trail of his wickedness and the evil end to which he leads, it is helpful to examine the direction of the good thoughts suggested to you. Look at their beginning and how little by little they made you fall away from the sweetness and spiritual joy you had, to the point where you went along with his depraved intentions. By recognising and noting such experience you can guard in future against these deceitful wiles.

[335] *Seventh rule.* As for those who are progressing to greater perfection, the good angel touches their souls sweetly and gently like a drop of water seeping into a sponge. The evil angel taps them sharply, with noise and disturbance, like a drop of water hitting a rock. But those who are going from bad to worse are touched in the opposite manner by the above spirits. The reason for this is based on whether the soul's disposition is the opposite or the same as that of the spirits. When the soul has the opposite disposition to the spirits they enter noisily and with commotion, but when it is the same, the spirits enter silently as if entering a house through open doors.

[336] *Eighth rule.* When you receive a consolation unexpectedly, although we know that this means that it comes directly from God our Lord, you should be very vigilant and take care to distinguish the consolation itself from the feeling of warmth and comfort that remains in the soul after the consolation has passed. Often during this second stage, through using your own ideas and judgements you may, at the instigation of the good or evil spirit, form other intentions and suggestions that are not given immediately by God our Lord. Therefore they must be examined very carefully before you approve them entirely or put them into effect.

[337] RULES FOR ALMSGIVING
In the ministry of distributing alms the following rules should be observed.

[338] *First rule.* If I distribute anything to relations or friends, or to people I am fond of, I must observe four things, which have been mentioned in part under the subject of the Choice. The first is that the love that moves me and makes me give the alms must come down from above, from the love of God our Lord, so that I feel primarily that God is the motive of the greater or lesser love I have for these people, and that God will be glorified more if I love them more.

[339] *Second rule.* I must think about a person whom I have never seen or known. I want him to have total perfection in the ministry and state he is in. I want him to be wise in the way he gives alms for the greater glory of God our Lord and the greater perfection of his soul. Then I must do likewise, neither more nor less. I keep the rule and measure I decided on and judged to be right for this other person.

[340] *Third rule*. I should consider what rule and measure I would want to have observed in my almsgiving, if I were at the point of death. I should be guided by this and follow this rule in my actual almsgiving.

[341] *Fourth rule*. I should imagine myself at the day of judgement and think how I would wish to have fulfilled this office and carried out this ministry. The rule that I would wish to have observed then, I should keep now.

[342] *Fifth rule*. If you feel well disposed and affectionate towards certain people, to whom you want to give alms, pause and mull over the above four rules, examining and testing your affection through them. Do not give any alms until any disordered affection you feel has been brought into line with these rules.

[343] *Sixth rule*. It is not wrong to take gifts from God our Lord to distribute them to others, when you are called by God our Lord to such a ministry. But there is a risk of wrongdoing and excess in the matter of how much you take and use for yourself and what you should give to others. Therefore you should reform and live your life according to the above rules.

[344] *Seventh rule*. For the reasons already mentioned and for many others, in matters regarding personal wealth and quality of house, it is always better and safer, the more it is restricted and cut down, and the closer we come to our supreme high priest, our pattern and norm, who is Christ our Lord. This is in line with the ruling of the Third Council of Carthage (at which St Augustine was present) that the furniture of a bishop should be common and poor. The same rule should be followed in all walks of life, taking into account the person's social position. In marriage, for instance, we have the example of St Joachim and St Anne, who divided their possessions into three parts. They gave the first part to the poor, the second to the ministry and service of the temple and kept the third to maintain themselves and their family.

[345] NOTES CONCERNING SCRUPLES
The following notes are useful for discerning and understanding scruples and the tricks of our enemy.

[346] *First note*. Scruple is the name which is commonly given to what really comes from our own judgement and freedom. I may freely make something out to be a sin, which is not a sin. For example, this happens when someone accidentally treads on a cross made of straws and decides in his own judgement that he has sinned. This is strictly speaking an error of judgement and not a real scruple.

[347] *Second note*. After I have trodden on this cross, or after I have thought or said or done some other thing, the thought comes to me from the outside that I have sinned. Although on the other hand I may feel I have not sinned, nevertheless I feel disturbed about it and am in two minds. This really is a scruple and a temptation suggested by the enemy.

[348] *Third note*. The scruple mentioned in the first note is not to be given any credit because it is completely wrong. But the one in the second note can be usefully entertained for a while by a person doing spiritual exercises. It purges the soul and rids it of sin. This is in accordance with the saying of St Gregory: 'It is the mark of good souls to see a fault even where there is no fault.'

[349] *Fourth note*. The enemy observes very closely whether the soul is dull or sensitive. If it is sensitive he refines it even more, in order to disturb and defeat it. For example, if he sees that a soul will not consciously tolerate any deliberate sin, whether mortal or venial, then if he cannot make the soul fall into something that seems to be a sin, he tries to make the soul see a sin where there is no sin. For example, in a slight word or thought. If the soul is dull the enemy tries to make it duller. For example, if it used to take no notice of venial sins, the enemy tries to make it also take little notice of mortal sins. If it took some notice before, the enemy now makes it take much less notice or none.

[350] *Fifth note*. The soul that wants to make progress in the spiritual life must always go in the opposite direction to the enemy. That is, if the enemy wants to make the soul dull, the soul must try to refine itself. Likewise if the enemy is trying to refine the soul to extremes, the soul must try to become more solid, so that it can become calmer.

[351] *Sixth note*. When a devout soul wants to speak or do something not contrary to the Church or to the mind of superiors, that is to the glory of the Lord our God, and a thought or temptation comes from

outside, not to speak or do that thing, giving apparent reasons such as avoiding pride etc., then you should raise your mind to your Creator and Lord. If you see that this is a proper way to serve him, or at least not improper, you should go against the temptation. St Bernard answered a similar temptation with the words: 'I did not undertake this because of you and I am not going to abandon it because of you.'

[352] RULES FOR THINKING WITH THE CHURCH
In order to think with the Church militant we should keep the following rules.

[353] *First rule.* Putting aside all private judgement, we should keep our minds prepared and ready to obey the true bride of Christ our Lord in everything. This is our holy Mother, the hierarchical Church.

[354] *Second rule.* We should praise confession to a priest and receive the most holy sacrament once a year, or even better once a month, or better still every week, observing the necessary conditions.

[355] *Third rule.* We should praise the frequent hearing of Mass, also songs, psalms and long prayers both in and out of church. Likewise, the hours ordained for the divine office and for prayer of every kind and all canonical hours.

[356] *Fourth rule.* We should greatly praise religious orders, virginity and celibacy, but not praise marriage as much as any of these.

[357] *Fifth rule.* We should praise vows of religion, obedience, poverty and chastity and other works of perfection. Since a vow is taken upon matters connected with evangelical perfection, we should not make a vow about matters not connected with it, such as to go into business, get married etc.

[358] *Sixth rule.* We should esteem relics of saints, and venerate them and pray to the saints. We should praise the station churches, pilgrimages, indulgences, pardons, crusades and candles lit in churches.

[359] *Seventh rule.* We should praise rulings by the Church on fasting and abstinence, such as Lent, Ember days, Vigils, Fridays and Saturdays. Likewise we should observe not only interior but also exterior penances.

[360] *Eighth rule*. We should praise ornaments and church buildings and images, and venerate them according to what they represent.

[361] *Ninth rule*. Finally we should praise all the Church's precepts, being alert to defend her and in no way to attack her.

[362] *Tenth rule*. We should be prompt to approve and praise the Church's rulings and recommendations and also the way of acting of our superiors. Although some of them may not be or may not have been praiseworthy, speaking against them, either by preaching in public or by frequently speaking about them in front of people, would cause more grumbling and scandal than benefit. Then the people would become angry at their superiors, either secular or spiritual. Nevertheless, although it does harm to speak ill of superiors in their absence to the people, it can do good to speak to the persons themselves about their bad conduct, so that they can remedy it.

[363] *Eleventh rule*. We should praise the teaching of the Fathers and the Scholastics. For the patristic doctors like St Jerome, St Augustine and St Gregory move the affections to love and serve God our Lord in all things, whereas the Scholastics, such as St Thomas, St Bonaventure and the Master of the Sentences define and explain for us today things that are necessary to our eternal salvation. They lead in attacking and exposing all errors and fallacies. For the Scholastic doctors, being more modern, not only take advantage of the true understanding of Holy Scripture and the holy patristic doctors, they are also enlightened by the divine power and have the help of the councils, canons and constitutions of our Holy Mother the Church.

[364] *Twelfth rule*. We must guard against making comparisons between ourselves who are alive now and the blessed souls in the past. Great error is committed here. For example, when someone says, 'This man knows more than St Augustine or more than St Francis, he is another St Paul in goodness, holiness,' and so on.

[365] *Thirteenth rule*. We should always be ready to believe that the white I see is black, if the Church says so. We should believe that between Christ our Lord the bridegroom and the Church his bride there is one and the same Spirit who governs and rules us for the

salvation of our souls. For our Holy Mother the Church is ruled and governed by the same Spirit and our Lord who gave the ten commandments.

[366] *Fourteenth rule.* Although it is very true that no one can be saved without being predestined, and without having faith and grace, we must be very careful how we speak and treat these subjects.

[367] *Fifteenth rule.* We should not make a habit of speaking much about predestination. When we do speak about it, it should be done in such a way that ordinary people are not led astray. Or else they may conclude: If I am predestined to be saved or damned, the question is already determined, and doing good or evil will not alter the end result. Then they become insolent and neglect good works that lead to the salvation and spiritual benefit of their souls.

[368] *Sixteenth rule.* Likewise, we must be careful not to speak too much or too enthusiastically about faith, without explaining what we are saying. We should not give the people cause to become sluggardly and lazy in good works, whether before or after they have faith informed by charity.

[369] *Seventeenth rule.* Likewise, we should not talk about grace so much and so enthusiastically that it gives room to the poisonous teaching that excludes free will. We may speak about faith and grace, insofar as God helps us, and so long as it is to the praise of his Divine Majesty. But in these dangerous days we should not speak about grace in such a way that good deeds and free will are in any way disparaged or discounted.

[370] *Eighteenth rule.* Although we must serve God our Lord diligently out of pure love, we must also greatly praise the fear of his Divine Majesty. Not only filial respect is a pious and most holy thing, so is servile fear. For, when a person has not attained anything better or more useful, it can help greatly in liberation from mortal sin. And when we have got rid of sin we will be able to feel filial respect, which is wholly acceptable and pleasing to God our Lord because it is inseparable from the love of God.